PRELUDE:
What If?

What if life were perfect?

What if you lived in a perfect world of perfect people and perfect possessions, with everyone and everything doing the perfect thing at the perfect time?

What if you had everything you wanted, and only what you wanted, exactly as you wanted, precisely when you wanted it?

What if, after luxuriating in this perfect world for the perfect length of time, you started feeling uneasy about the predictability of perfection?

What if, after a perfect length of additional time, you began thinking, "There seems to be a lack of risk, adventure and fun in perfection. 'Having it my way' all the time is starting to get dull."

What if, after yet another perfect length of time, you decided, "Perfection is a perfect bore."

What if, at that point in your perfect world, you noticed for the first time a button marked, "Surprise."

What if you walked over, considered all that might be contained in the concept of "surprise," decided, "Anything's better than perfect boredom," took a deep breath, pushed the button...

...and found yourself where you are right now—feeling what you're feeling now, thinking what you're thinking now, with everything in your life precisely the way it is now—reading this book.

*The essence of our effort to
see that every child has a
chance must be to assure
each an equal opportunity,
not to become equal,
but to become different—
to realize whatever unique
potential of body, mind and
spirit he or she possesses.*

JOHN FISCHER

LIFE 101

Everything We Wish We Had Learned About Life In School —But Didn't

by
John-Roger and Peter McWilliams

PRELUDE PRESS
8165 Mannix Drive
Los Angeles, California 90046

A Bantam-Prelude Book
Published simultaneously in the United States and Canada

Bantam Books are published by Bantam Books, a division of Bantam Doubleday Dell Publishing Group, Inc. Its trademark, consisting of the words "Bantam Books" and the portrayal of a rooster, is Registered in U.S. Patent and Trademark Office and in other countries. Marca Registrada. Bantam Books, 666 Fifth Avenue, New York, New York 10103

Printed in the United States of America

Book and Cover Design: Paul LeBus

Editorial Consultants: Leigh S. Fortson, Ed Fortson, Bernice Stangrover, Victoria Marine

Photography: Betty Bennett

Desktop Publishing: Richard Carson, John & Jack Moran, Sara J. Thomas

If your local bookstore is out, you may order additional copies by calling:

1-800-LIFE-101

*At college age, you can tell
who is best at taking tests
and going to school,
but you can't tell who
the best people are.
That worries the hell
out of me.*

BARNABY C. KEENEY

CONTENTS

PART TWO
ADVANCED TOOLS FOR EAGER LEARNERS

PART THREE
MASTER TEACHERS

PART FOUR
TOOLS FOR

PART FIVE
TO HAVE JOY AND TO HAVE
IT MORE ABUNDANTLY

*This book is dedicated
to all who are living life.*

LIFE 101

**Everything We Wish We Had
Learned About Life In School
—But Didn't**

*Only the curious
will learn and
only the resolute overcome
the obstacles to learning.
The quest quotient has
always excited me more
than the intelligence
quotient.*

EUGENE S. WILSON

PART ONE

INTRODUCTION TO LIFE

Welcome to life.

We call this book *LIFE 101* because it contains all the things we wish we had learned about life in school but, for the most part, did not.

After twelve (or more) years of schooling, we know how to figure the square root of an isosceles triangle (invaluable in daily life), but we might not know how to forgive ourselves and others (and the value of that).

We know what direction migrating birds fly in autumn, but we're not sure which way we want to go.

We have dissected a frog, but perhaps have never explored the dynamics of human relationships.

We know who wrote, "To be or not to be, that is the question," but we don't know the answer.

We know what pi is, but we're not sure who we are.

We may know how to diagram a sentence, but we may not know how to love ourselves.

That our educational system is not designed to teach us the "secrets of life" is no secret. In school, we learn how to do everything—except how to live.

Maybe that's the way it should be. Unraveling life's "mysteries" and discovering life's "secrets" (which are, in fact, neither mysterious nor secretive) may take the courage and determination found only in a self-motivated pursuit.

Fred Sanford: Didn't you learn anything being my son? Who do you think I'm doing this all for?

Lamont Sanford: Yourself.

Fred: Yeah, you learned something.

Since you've picked up a book with the title *LIFE 101*, it seems safe to assume that you have at least a passing interest in the subject of life. You probably already know there's more to life than reading, 'riting and 'rithmetic.

We're glad you learned reading, of course, or you wouldn't be able to read this book. We're also glad we learned 'riting (such as it is). And 'rithmetic? Well, as Mae West once said, "One and one is two, two and two are four, and five will get you ten if you know how to work it."

That's what this book is about: knowing how to work it, and having fun along the way.

If it's not fun, we're not interested.

Although a lot can be learned from adversity, most of the same lessons can be learned through laughter and joy. If you're anything like us, you've probably had more than enough adversity. (Most people, once they graduate from the School of Hard Knocks, automatically enroll in the University of Adversity.)

We are *sincere* about life, but we're not *serious* about it. If you're looking for serious, pedantic, didactic instruction, you will not find it here. We will—with a light heart —present hundreds of techniques and suggestions, and for each of them we make the same suggestion:

Give it a try.

If it works for you, fine—use it; it's yours. If it doesn't work for you, let it go and move onto something that does.

Not everything in *LIFE 101* will be for you. We're laying out a smorgasbord. The carrot-raisin salad you pass up may be the very thing another person craves, and the caviar you're making a beeline for might be just so much salty black stuff to the carrot-salad lover.

If we say something you find not "true," please don't discount everything else in the book. It may be "true" for someone else. That same someone else might say, "What nonsense," over something, while you knowingly mutter, "How true." It's a large world, and life has many truths. Take what you can use and leave the rest.

*We don't receive wisdom;
we must discover it
for ourselves after a journey
that no one can take for us
or spare us.*

MARCEL PROUST

If you take ten percent—any ten percent—and use it as your own, we'll consider our job more than well done.

Which brings us to the question: Who is the *real* teacher of *LIFE 101?* We'll get to that shortly. (Hint: It's not us.)

For now, welcome to *LIFE 101.* When you were born, you probably had quite a welcome, but you may have been too young to remember it. So, as you begin this "life," please feel welcome.

Although it may be "just a book," it's a book of ideas from our minds to yours; a book of best wishes from our hearts to yours. If you catch the spirit of that, you'll see that our time together can be an intimate and loving one.

Welcome.

Life is far too important a thing ever to talk about.

OSCAR WILDE

Why Life?

What's it all about? Why are we here? What's the point? *Is* there a point? Why bother?

Why life?

At some point, you have probably pondered The Meaning of Life, and you came up with a satisfactory answer, which either has or has not stood the test of time, or you shrugged mightily, muttered, "Beats the hell out of me," and ordered a cheeseburger.

The question which precedes "What's the meaning of life?" is, of course, "*Is there* a meaning to life?" Beats the hell out of us. We're going to explore the first question *as though* the answer to the second question is yes.

If it's true that life has no meaning—no purpose—then it doesn't matter whether we've consumed a few pages speculating on the meaning of life. In fact, if there is no purpose to life, *nothing* matters. It's like trying to play a game with no rules, no boundaries, no nets, no teams and no scoring system—just five billion players.

So let's start the game by *assuming* there is a purpose to life. Our question then becomes, "*If there is* a purpose to life, what is it?"

Here's our answer (which we'll explore in the next three chapters):

Life is for doing, learning and enjoying.

Things won are done;
joy's soul lies in the doing.

SHAKESPEARE

Doing

One thing about humans: we are *doing* creatures. We always seem to be doing something. When we're not doing something, we're *thinking* about doing something, which, of course, is doing something. When we sleep, we toss and dream. We do exercises to keep our bodies in shape so we can do even more.

Humans are well designed for doing. Unlike trees, our bodies can move from place to place. Our emotions can move from happy to sad, and back again, in a matter of minutes. Our thoughts move us to places we can't go physically: our memory moves us back in time, our intelligence anticipates future movement, and our imagination moves us to places we've never been.

We also do *to* nature—you name it, and humans have either moved it or done something to it. (At the very least, we named it.) We seem bent on rearranging the world. We invent tools to move that which we cannot move with our bodies alone.

The successful theatrical director, Moss Hart, had a country home. He would visit on weekends, and request of his landscape designer that a few trees be put over there, a stream over here, and please move that mountain a few hundred feet to the left. The playwright George S. Kaufman visited Hart's home and remarked, "This is the way God would do it if He only had money."

It's often been observed that, from afar, the doing of humans resembles the frantic bustling of ants. We must occasionally wonder, "What is the purpose of all this doing?" We are not, after all, rocks, which don't seem to do much at all. We were obviously given the ability to do, but why?

We must, of course, do in order to meet our bodily needs (which would not be as great if we did not do as much), but even after these needs are met, we keep on doing. Why? Our suggestion:

Our doing allows for more learning.

Wear your learning,
like your watch,
in a private pocket:
and do not pull it out
and strike it,
merely to show
that you have one.

EARL OF CHESTERFIELD
1774

Learning is not
attained by chance,
it must be sought for with ardor
and attended to with diligence.

ABIGAIL ADAMS
1780

Learning

Life is for learning? Learning what? You name it. There's a lot to learn. In the first five years alone we learned physical coordination, walking, talking, eating, going potty, interaction with family and playmates, a great many facts about this planet, and all the other things that differentiate a five-year-old from a newly born infant.

From five to ten we learned reading, writing, arithmetic, geography, history, science, music, sports—and when we weren't watching television we learned some more about people: friends, relatives, enemies, allies, rivals, supporters, detractors.

And so learning continued. Some of what we learned early on turned out to be true (the earth is round; if you want a friend, be a friend; cleanliness is next to impossible) and some of it turned out to be false (Santa Claus; the Tooth Fairy; Kansas is more fun than Oz).

Some things had to be relearned—or unlearned—and while relearning and unlearning, maybe we learned what to do about disappointment—and maybe we didn't.

Looking back on most people's lives, we see dramatic growth until the age of fifteen or twenty. Then the growing slows, stops or, in some cases, regresses.

What happens is that most people declare themselves "done" when their formal education is over. What is it about renting a cap and gown and a scroll of paper that makes us think our learning days are over?

It's not that there's nothing left to learn. Far from it. "Commencement" does not just mean graduation; it means a new beginning.

The more we learn, the more we can do. The more we do, the more we can learn. But in all this doing and learning, let's not forget one of the most important lessons of all—enjoyment.

Seek not, my soul,
the life of the immortals;
but enjoy to the full
the resources
that are within thy reach.

PINDAR
518-438 B.C.

How good is man's life,
the mere living!
How fit to employ all the heart
and the soul and the senses
forever in joy!

ROBERT BROWNING
1855

Enjoying

Joy is an interesting word. It does not have an automatic opposite created by grafting "un" or "dis" or "in" to it. There is: pleasure and displeasure, happiness and unhappiness, gratitude and ingratitude—but there is no unjoy, disjoy or injoy. (Can you imagine the word inenjoy?)

Joy seems to be something that can take place no matter what else is going on, no matter what other thoughts are being thought, no matter what other feelings or physical sensations are being felt.

The old story comes to mind: Two brothers went to ride ponies on their uncle's ranch, but first the uncle insisted that they shovel a large pile of manure out of a stall. One brother hated the project, and grumbled his way through a few halfhearted scoops. The other brother was laughing and singing and shoveling with abandon. "What are you so happy about?" the first brother asked. "Well," the second replied, "with all this manure, there must be a pony in here someplace!"

So it is with life. When life seems truly, um, excremental, we can moan and groan over our fate, or we can —even in the midst of anger, terror, confusion and pain— tell ourselves, "There must be a lesson in here someplace!"

Learn to enjoy the process of learning.

In those times when there's not much to learn, you can learn to enjoy the enjoyment. As Confucius observed 2,500 years ago, "With coarse rice to eat, with water to drink, and my bended arm for a pillow—I have still joy in the midst of these things." Or, as Thorton Wilder pointed out, "Enjoy your ice cream while it's on your plate—that's my philosophy."

Joy might be, in fact, not just something to enjoy while learning lessons; it may also be a technique for learning some of the most profound lessons of all. "With an eye made quiet by the power of harmony, and the deep power of joy," Wordsworth wrote, "we see into the life of things."

*A man's life of any worth
is a continual allegory.*

JOHN KEATS

Life Is a Metaphor

There are many models for life: analogies, allegories and metaphors to help us understand something as complicated, intricate and seemingly *un*understandable as life.

There is the Life Is a Game school of thought (and its many subschools: Life Is a Baseball Game, Life Is a Football Game, Life Is Like Tennis, Life Is Chess, Life Is Monopoly, Life As Croquet).

"Life is like a game of whist," Eugene Hare pointed out some time ago. "From unseen sources the cards are shuffled, and the hands are dealt." Later, Josh Billings completed the thought: "Life consists not in holding good cards but in playing those you hold well."

Some believe Life Is an Intricate Machine (very popular in Germany). In northern California they believe Life Is a Computer. Buckminster Fuller synthesized the two, "The earth is like a spaceship that didn't come with an operating manual."

Is life work or is life play? Karl Marx said, "Living is working," and Henry Ford, of all people, agreed. ("Life is work.") Disagreeing is Leon de Montenaeken, who said, "Life is but play," and Liza de Minnelli, who sang, "Life is a cabaret."

Seneca said, "Life is a play. It's not its length, but its performance that counts." What kind of play is it? Jean de La Bruyere suggested life's "a tragedy for those who feel, a comedy for those who think." Kirk Douglas called life "a B-picture script." (From Seneca to Kirk Douglas in one paragraph. Not bad.)

Shakespeare, of course, called life "A player that struts and frets its hour upon the stage..." and James Thurber continued: "It's a tale told in an idiom, full of unsoundness and fury, signifying nonism." George Bernard Shaw also took the Bard to task: "Life is no brief candle to me. It is sort of a splendid torch that I have got hold of for the moment."

*The very purpose of
existence is to reconcile the
glowing opinion we hold of
ourselves with the appalling
things that other people
think about us.*

QUENTIN CRISP

There are those who like musical analogies. "Life is something like a trumpet," W. C. Handy pointed out, "If you don't put anything in, you won't get anything out." Samuel Butler said, "Life is playing a violin solo in public and learning the instrument as one goes on." Ella Wheeler Wilcox sang: "Our lives are songs: God writes the words / and we set them to music at pleasure; / and the song grows glad, or sweet or sad / as we choose to fashion the measure."

One of the nicest literary analogies comes from the Jewish Theological Seminary: "A life is a single letter in the alphabet. It can be meaningless. Or it can be part of a great meaning."

One of the greatest letters in the American alphabet, Helen Keller, proclaimed, "Life is either a daring adventure, or nothing." George Bernard Shaw, in his own way, agreed: "Life is a series of inspired follies. The difficulty is to find them to do. Never lose a chance: it doesn't come every day."

If we've been too esoteric in our references, let's get back to earth. How about closing this chapter with the Life Is Food contingent?

"Life is an onion," Carl Sandburg wrote, "You peel it off one layer at a time, and sometimes you weep." "Life is like eating artichokes," T. A. Dorgan tells us, "you've got to go through so much to get so little." Or maybe it's more as Auntie Mame pointed out, "Life is a banquet, and some poor sons-of-bitches are starving."

Don Marquis called life "a scrambled egg." Make of that what you will—but then, we could say that about life itself, couldn't we?

And what do *we* think life is? What model do we use to describe our time together? Please turn the page.

*Universities should be safe
havens where ruthless
examination of realities
will not be
distorted by
the aim to please
or inhibited
by the risk of displeasure.*

KINGMAN BREWSTER

Life Is a Classroom

It should come as no surprise that, if we think life is for learning, we would view the process of life itself as a classroom. But it's not a dull, sit-in-neat-little-rows-and-listen-to-some-puffed-up-professor-drone-on-and-on classroom. It is (as we're sure you've noticed) highly experiential. In that sense, life's more of a workshop.

We like to think the workshop/classroom of life is perfectly arranged so that we learn what we need to know, when we need to know it, in precisely the way we need to learn it.

The operative word in all that is *need*, not *want*.

We don't always learn what we *want* to learn when we want to learn it. In tenth grade biology there was only one animal's reproductive methods we were interested in studying, but we had to start with splitting of amoebas and work our way up. Thank heaven for *Playboy* and *Cosmopolitan*.

The biology teacher had a lesson plan different from ours. And so, it seems, does life.

Life's lessons come in all shapes and sizes. Just as in school, the most important lessons sometimes come in nonformal learning situations. Some days you probably learned more in the five minutes between classes than during the fifty-five minutes of official class time.

Sometimes what we need to know we learn in a formal way, such as taking a class or reading a book. Sometimes we learn by an informal, seemingly accidental process: an overheard comment in an elevator, a friend's offhand remark, or the line of a song from a passing radio ("Don't worry, be happy").

We like to think there are no accidents.

Positive lessons are not always taught in positive ways. A flat tire (hardly a positive occurrence, unless it's somebody else's tire and you own a tire store) can teach any number of lessons: acceptance, the value of planning, patience, the joy of service (if another person has the flat

*The most important
function of education
at any level is to develop
the personality of the
individual and the
significance of his life to
himself and to others.
This is the basic
architecture of a life;
the rest is ornamentation
and decoration of
the structure.*

GRAYSON KIRK

tire), the gratitude of being served (if another person helps you), and so on.

We can also use the same flat tire to learn (or relearn, or rerelearn, or rererelearn) depressing lessons: life isn't fair; nothing can be trusted; if anything can go wrong it will at the worst possible moment; life's a pain —then you die; nobody loves me; etc.

Do you begin to see your role in all this? The classroom of life is not third grade, where every subject and what you will learn each day is fully planned—including recess. You *choose* what you learn from the many lessons presented to you, and your *choice* is fundamental to what you actually learn.

There are any number of lessons—both uplifting and "downpushing"—we can learn from any experience in life.

Experience, it is said, is the best teacher—providing, of course, we become the best students.

But who, really, is the teacher?

*We learn simply by the
exposure of living.
Much that passes for
education is not education
at all but ritual.
The fact is that we are
being educated when
we know it least.*

DAVID P. GARDNER

Who Is the Real Teacher?

The real teacher of life is not experience. It's not over-heard conversations or lines from songs or what you read in books (or the people who wrote the books).

The real teacher is *you*. You're the one who must decide, of all that comes your way, what is true and what is not, what applies to you and what does not, what you learn now and what you promise yourself you'll learn later.

Have you noticed that two people can read the same book or see the same movie or take the same course and remember entirely different things? The best that life can do is *present* lessons to you. The learning is up to you.

The two of us can't do any better than life. All we can do is present certain points of view, possible explanations, and whatever we (and some of our friends) have learned from certain experiences.

From what we present, it's up to you to say, "Yes, that fits," "No, that doesn't," or "Let me work with it for a while and I'll see." If it fits, take it: it's yours. We just put words around something you already knew.

If you listen carefully, you'll hear (or sense) a voice inside yourself. It's the voice of your inner teacher. (We'll use the word voice, but for you it may be an image or a feeling or a sensation or any combination of these.) It may not be the loudest voice "in there," but it's often the most consistent, patient and persistent one.

What does your inner teacher sound like? It's the one that just said, "I sound like this."

If you're like us, you probably had other voices answering that question, too. "No, no, I sound like this." "There is no inner voice." "More than one voice? Do they think I'm crazy?" "Inner teacher. How stupid!"

But, through the din—lovingly, calmly, and perhaps a little amused by all the commotion caused by a simple question—the inner teacher reminds you:

"I am here. I have always been here. I'm on your side. I love you."

*Nobody can be
exactly like me.
Sometimes even I
have trouble doing it.*

TALLULAH BANKHEAD

Who Are You? Who *Are* You?
Who Are *You?*

What are all those other voices? Who's saying all that stuff? And why? And which "you" do we mean when we say, "*You* are the real teacher?"

Try a brief experiment. Take a moment and be aware of your body. Quickly "scan" it from your feet to your head. How does it feel? Are there any areas of tightness or tension? Do any parts feel particularly good? Is there any soreness or stiffness? Do you feel tired or alert?

Now, take a look at your emotions. (Or maybe we should say, "Take a feel of your emotions.") What are you feeling? Excitement? Fear? Contentment? Irritability? Calmness? Feelings are often felt in and around the heart (the center of the chest) and the stomach. What are you feeling there?

One more bit of observation: notice your thoughts. What thoughts are you thinking? Listen to your mind as it goes through its thought process. Someone once clocked the speed of human thinking and said that we think at 1,200 words per minute. How they counted them, we don't know. How they translated the visual and sensory thinking we do into words, we also don't know. That figure does, however, give a sense of the "chattering" we do inside our heads. Listen to the chatter for a moment.

Thank you. Now, one question: Who did all that? Who noticed the body? Who felt the feelings? Who observed the mind?

Maybe it was something other than—greater than—the body, greater than the emotions, greater than the mind.

Maybe it was *you*.

*The body is a community
made up of its innumerable
cells or inhabitants.*

THOMAS ALVA EDISON

Maybe You Are More than Your Body

The body has enormous wisdom: it circulates your blood, digests your food, and performs thousands of necessary functions every second—without your ever having to "think" about them.

The body keeps itself from getting ill and heals itself when it does. It sees, hears, feels, tastes, smells—and has the sense to do that without ever being taught how. And it performs the amazing feat of balancing the entire body on two legs, something—considering its size, proportions and center of gravity—it has no business doing.

Alas, the body, as remarkable as it is, doesn't have much "smarts." Instincts, absolutely. Nonhuman animals have bodies, too, complete with wisdom and instincts. But something, whatever it is—reason, intelligence, awareness, soul or "smarts"—separates humans from the rest of the animal kingdom.

Ask yourself: are you (the *you* you) located in the body, or located in the "something extra"? That's a loaded question, of course. Who can resist the temptation to associate themselves with the "something extra" (especially a *mysterious* something extra)?

Even unloading the question ("Are you more than your physical body?"), we think you see the point:

As remarkable as our bodies are, we somehow know that we are more remarkable than that.

Crystal: Do you realize that most people use two percent of their mind's potential?

Roseanne: That much, huh?

ROSEANNE

Perhaps You Are More than Your Mind

This is a difficult concept for thinkers to think about, for comprehenders to comprehend. "The thing that separates the human from the beast is the human's superior intellect, its well-developed mind," they say.

Perhaps, perhaps not. Let's explore that a bit.

The mind is often too full of opinions and "facts" about the way things *were* to accurately evaluate the way things *are*. For many people, the mind's job is to prove that what it already knows is enough, and there's no need to learn anything new.

As John Kenneth Galbraith pointed out, "Faced with the choice between changing one's mind and proving there is no need to do so, almost everyone gets busy on the proof."

Firmness of mind, to a point, is a good thing. It keeps us from being wishy-washy, swayed by every new bit of information that comes our way. Carried beyond a certain point, however, the mind becomes closed to any new information from any source. The closed mind is, obviously, not open to learning. Learning is the assimilation and integration of new ideas, concepts and behaviors.

You may be wondering, "Is my mind closed?" If you're wondering that, it probably isn't. The closed mind, when faced with the concept that the mind is not the "It" of "Its," disregards the information, often vehemently. (As Dorothy Parker said, "This book is not to be tossed lightly aside, but to be hurled with great force.")

If you're still reading this book, and actively exploring the option that the mind might not be "you," then your mind is obviously open enough to accept the idea that it is not "It," and therefore open for learning.

Books such as *LIFE 101* have filters built in—not built into the book, necessarily, but into the people who might read the book. Those who are not open to new ideas seldom read a book that contains new ideas. They don't even pick one up. The title is reason enough to dis-

*Your mind must always go,
even while you're shaking
hands and going through
all the maneuvers.
I developed the ability long
ago to do one thing
while thinking another.*

RICHARD M. NIXON

1960

regard it. Their minds dismiss it with the generalization, "It's one of *those* books."

Even the section in the bookstore is enough. Some people never visit any of *those* sections. For some, the mere fact that it's a *book* is sufficient reason not to be bothered.

We don't mean to belittle the mind. The mind is an invaluable tool for sorting, organizing, conceptualizing and replaying information. The mind is a marvelous servant, it just makes a poor master.

*Joe, never feel guilty
about having
warm human feelings
toward anyone.*

BEN CARTWRIGHT
BONANZA

Possibly You Are More Than Your Emotions

Feelings are good things to have—when you're feeling good. There's nothing that feels quite so good as good feelings.

On the other hand, when feelings feel bad, we sometimes wish we didn't have feelings. If we use feelings to get us moving and change the thing that's causing the bad feelings so we can feel good again, then even the bad feelings are good. (More on this idea in Part Three: "Master Teachers in Disguise.")

Emotions are like the vibrations on the strings of a violin: They're essential to the song, but they're not the essence of the violin.

We experience life's pains and pleasures through our emotions. Because of this, some people decide they *are* their feelings. "I feel, therefore I am."

The problem is, emotions are too often too wrong to be who we truly are.

Did you ever feel you could trust somebody and you couldn't? Did you ever feel something bad was going to happen and it didn't? Did you ever feel you could spend the rest of your life loving someone, and, well, you know what happened to that one. (Or, more likely, you *don't* know what happened to that one.)

Our emotions are like yo-yo's: sometimes they're up, sometimes they're down. We can walk the dog, go 'round the world, or practice "sleeping." Yo-yo's are fun to play with, but who's holding the string?

If someone's holding the string, then "you" must be more than the string—be it the string of a violin, the strings of your heart, or the string of a yo-yo.

It's an
unanswered question,
but let us still believe in the
dignity and importance
of the question.

TENNESSEE WILLIAMS

So Who Are You?

If you're not your body, your mind or your emotions, who are you?

Some might say our sense of self is simply an amalgam of the three; that the interplay among the body, mind and emotions makes a whole that is greater than the sum of the parts, and that greater whole we call self.

This definition is fine with us, as are any religious, spiritual or metaphysical views of self you may have. (We'll get to all those—yes, all of them—in just a moment.)

We're not here to answer the question, "Who Are You?" We're here to suggest that there is a "You" to be discovered.

The discovery of that "You" is entirely your own—although the entire world will happily participate with you.

Jean-Paul Sartre
(arriving in heaven):
It's not what I expected.

God: *What did you expect?*

Sartre: *Nothing.*

SCTV

The Gap:
God, Religion, Reincarnation, Atheism, Agnosticism and All That

We're going to take a clear, unequivocal and unambiguous position on God, religion, reincarnation, atheism, agnosticism and all that. Our clear, unambiguous and unequivocal position is this: We are clearly, unambiguously and unequivocally *not* taking a position.

It's not that we don't *have* a point of view about each of these, it's just that the information in *LIFE 101* works regardless of our or your or anyone's point of view.

There are certain things—the pull of gravity, the need for breathing, the desire for ice cream—that affect all humans regardless of beliefs. *LIFE 101* concerns itself with those "belief-proof" issues.

We'd like to introduce a portion of life we call The Gap. The Gap is the area into which we put the many (often conflicting) beliefs people have about What's The Big Force Behind It All And How Does This Big Force Interact With Human Beings?

The Gap can be any size, large or small. For some, it's a hairline crack; for others, it's vast enough to hold universes. We are not here to comment on the contents of anyone's Gap. The contents of your Gap are between you and whomever or whatever is in your Gap.

We are not confirming, endorsing or supporting *any* point of view. Most people will find this statement liberating. "You mean I don't have to sort out The Gap before I sort out my life?" We don't think so. In fact, a sorted, prosperous, joyful life might make Gap exploration all the more fruitful.

There are some people, however, who have strong points of view on what should and should not be contained in everyone else's Gap. There are others who have powerful convictions concerning the lack of the Gap itself. Our militant wishy-washyism on this point will probably gather us some detractors from both extremes.

I love God, and when you get to know Him, you find He's a Livin' Doll.

JANE RUSSELL

One side might say: "I can't possibly read a book by people who do not categorically and emphatically state that there is a God, and believe in *my* God *my* way." We might ask these people if they've ever read a cookbook, road atlas or auto repair manual. These seldom state the theological convictions of the authors, but are read by the righteous every day.

The other extreme might say: "I can't even consider a book by people who are open to the idea that there is a God." We wonder if these people also investigate the beliefs of their doctor, dentist and mail delivery person—and refuse service if any of them happen to feel all right about the Almighty.

What *we* believe is giving people the freedom to believe whatever they choose to believe. The techniques contained in *LIFE 101* will help both believers and doubters —and everyone in between—to live a healthier, wealthier and happier life.

We'll be discussing techniques as direct and mechanical as cooking, car repair, map reading and mail delivery. Unlike cooking, car repair, map reading and mail delivery, however, the techniques for living a happier, healthier, more productive life have, in some cases, been linked to specific religious (or non-religious) beliefs.

What we're attempting to do in this chapter is to separate these techniques (which work regardless of belief or disbelief) from the claim that organized schools of thought —be they "religious" or "scientific"—have, at times, placed upon them.

The doctor who gives a vaccination and says, "Thank God, this child is safe from smallpox," and the doctor who gives a vaccination and says, "Thank Pasteur, this child is safe from smallpox," give the same vaccination. Some may say that the doctor who gives a blessing is a better doctor, and some may say that the doctor who sticks to medicine is a better doctor, but in either case—thank God and/or Pasteur—the child can be safe.

Historically, some "scientific" discoveries have been slow to be adopted by certain religious organizations, and some "mystical" techniques have taken some time to be adopted by science.

*My religion consists of a
humble admiration of the
illimitable superior spirit
who reveals himself in the
slight details we are able
to perceive with our
frail and feeble mind.*

ALBERT EINSTEIN

Do you think we're all "old enough" to set aside the source, history and trappings of certain techniques and ask of them a simple question: Do they work? (Do they produce the desired result? Do they get you what you want and need?)

In our combined three-quarters of a century of investigation, that's the underlying question we've asked. (Of course, it took a number of years to discover that was the question we should be asking. It's interesting that we can ask that question of itself, and it still holds up.)

So, as we go along, if we make a point that sounds like something you heard in Sunday School, that may be because you heard it in Sunday School. If we say something, and you think, "That sounds as though it came from the Ten Commandments," that may be because it came from the Ten Commandments. If you say, "There they go again, referring to Godless science," that's probably because we are referring, once again, to Godless science.

We don't just care where things come from; we also care where they might take us.

*Sooner or later every one of
us breathes an atom that
has been breathed before by
anyone you can think of
who has lived before us—
Michelangelo or
George Washington
or Moses.*

JACOB BRONOWSKI

There Is More Going On Than Our Senses Perceive

Our view of the world is primarily made up of what we have perceived through our five senses. What we *personally* know of the world we have either seen, touched, tasted, smelled or heard.

Unfortunately, our senses are limited, therefore our view of the world is limited. This is not a problem unless we start believing that what we perceive is all there is to be perceived. It is not.

This is disturbing news to those who believe, "If I can't see it, taste it, smell it, hear it or feel it, forget it."

If we were to tell you that, right now, there are hundreds of voices, pictures and songs filling the air around you, but you are unable to see or hear any of them, what would you think?

Would you think we were talking some metaphysical mumbo jumbo? "If there were hundreds of voices, pictures and songs around me, I'd be able to at least see or hear *some* of them."

Not necessarily.

"Then your explanation's going to be pretty weird."

Not necessarily that, either.

"Okay, so explain."

Right now you are surrounded by waves of energy...

"Sounds pretty weird already."

...that are used to transmit radio, television, walkie-talkie, CB, portable telephone and many other communication devices. The reason you don't know they're there is because your senses are unable to perceive these signals.

If you had a TV, however, you could use it to tune in these "waves of energy." The TV would translate what your senses cannot perceive into what they can. The fact that we can't see, hear or feel these waves without a TV

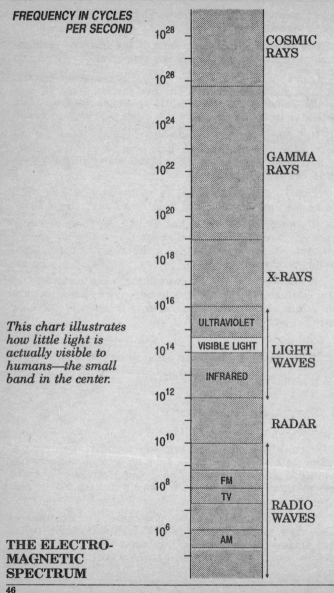

FREQUENCY IN CYCLES PER SECOND

This chart illustrates how little light is actually visible to humans—the small band in the center.

THE ELECTRO-MAGNETIC SPECTRUM

10^{28} — COSMIC RAYS

10^{26}

10^{24} — GAMMA RAYS

10^{22}

10^{20}

10^{18} — X-RAYS

10^{16} — ULTRAVIOLET

10^{14} — VISIBLE LIGHT / LIGHT WAVES

INFRARED

10^{12}

RADAR

10^{10}

10^{8} — FM

TV — RADIO WAVES

10^{6}

AM

doesn't mean they're not there. They are; we're just not able to perceive them.

And thus it is with all sorts of natural and human-made phenomena. If we have the proper instruments, we can perceive them. If not, we are mostly unaware of their existence.

Dogs smell and hear better than most humans. Cats see better in the dark. Birds are more sensitive to movement. Even flies seem to "know" when you're about to swat them.

The point is a simple one: There is more to life than meets the eye.

Man is slightly nearer to the atom than to the star. From his central position man can survey the grandest works of Nature with the astronomer, or the minutest works with the physicist.

SIR ARTHUR STANLEY

Life Is Energy

Before we put life together the way we'd like it, let's break it down into its component parts—or, maybe, part.

Mystics and sages of old maintained that this hard, material life is really just energy—vibrations that vibrate in certain ways that appear to our limited senses as solid forms.

The "materialists" of those ancient times (science, as such, had not yet been invented) scoffed. They knew a club upside the head hurt, and a rock was a lot harder than mere "vibrations."

A few millennia later, about 2,500 years ago, the Greeks proposed that all life was made of atoms (*atomos* means "indivisible" in Greek), and that atoms were made of energy. Hence, physics was born. (The term physics comes from the Greek word *physis*, the attempt to see the essential nature of things.)

Some said of this theory, "Life is energy. Of course." Others said, "Life is energy? Prove it." So the physicists went about proving it. Unfortunately, the tools for proving it were too crude to prove anything of the kind. The proof, in fact, supported the idea that life was not energy, but was little bits of very solid stuff.

Hence, the rift between faith and science deepened. The faithful could not "prove" life was energy, and the tools of science were too crude to prove that life was anything but solid matter.

The gap continued to widen until the early 1900's, when Einstein proved mathematically (another awfully hard science) that energy is matter. ($E=mc^2$—Energy equals matter times the speed of light, squared.)

Physicists now had a formula by which they could design the machinery to look at the subtler workings of the universe.

They found that atoms were, on the one hand, much smaller than originally thought, and, on the other hand, much bigger.

*A physicist is an atom's way
of knowing about atoms.*

GEORGE WALD

To give you an idea of how small an atom is, imagine a cherry. Then imagine trillions and trillions of cherries, all in one enormous ball. Imagine a ball the size of the earth, all made up of cherries. (If someone out there thinks we are about to make a terrible pun, such as "Life is just a ball of cherries"—or any comment whatsoever about such a world being the pits—you are mistaken.)

This large ball of cherries the size of the earth would be a fairly accurate model of the atomic structure of an orange. That is, if you enlarged an orange until it was the size of the earth, the atoms in that very big orange would be the size of cherries.

Another example of an atom's smallness: pure gold can be pounded very thin. When pounded extremely thin, it's known as gold leaf. Gold leaf is about five gold atoms thick. If this book, and three others just as thick, were printed on gold leaf, the total thickness of all four books would be about as thick as a single sheet of paper.

That's how small atoms are. But atoms are also surprisingly *large*.

Remember those models of atoms they showed us in school? They looked like little solar systems. (In some schools, they probably used the same model for both atoms *and* solar systems.) In the middle were the protons and neutrons; this, the teacher explained, formed the nucleus. Then, only slightly smaller than the nucleus, and about twelve inches away, dangling at the end of what looked like coat-hanger wire, was the electron.

These proportions are, to say the least, inaccurate. If the nucleus of the atom were, say, the size of a tennis ball, the electron would be from one to ten *miles* away (depending on the size of the atom). If the nucleus were the size of a tennis ball, the atom would be from two to twenty miles in diameter.

In the models we were shown at school, the electron hanging at the end of the coat-hanger wire was about the same size as the nucleus. An electron, in fact, is much, much smaller than the nucleus: about 2,000 times smaller. In our more accurate model, if the nucleus were the size of a tennis ball, the electron would hardly be visible.

*The important thing in science is
not so much to obtain new facts
as to discover new ways
of thinking about them.*

SIR WILLIAM BRAGG

*The most incomprehensible thing
about the world is that
it is comprehensible.*

ALBERT EINSTEIN

To give you another example of the size: Imagine the dome of St. Peter's Cathedral in Rome. (If you haven't been to St. Peter's, imagine the biggest dome you have seen and make it bigger.) If an atom were the size of St. Peter's dome, the nucleus would be the size of a grain of salt, and the electron would be smaller than a fleck of dust.

But what electrons lack in size they make up for in *speed*. They whiz about the nucleus at the rate of almost 600 miles per second. When you imagine how many times around the nucleus an electron needs to travel to make just one mile, multiply that times 600, and imagine that this goes on every second, you can begin to see how the electron pulls off its illusion.

Illusion? Sure. The electron moves so quickly around the nucleus that it gives the *illusion* of a solid shell. If you ever moved a flashlight back and forth in the dark, you know how it forms the illusion of a straight line. If you move the flashlight in a circle, it gives the illusion of a circle. This is what the speedy electron does as it zips around the nucleus.

An atom with a nucleus the size of a grain of salt *appears to be* the size of St. Peter's dome. The nucleus is 99.95 percent of the mass ("solid stuff") of the atom. The rest of the atom is nothing, appearing to be much, much bigger (a grain of salt pretending to be a dome) because of the whizzing electron. (The protons and neutrons don't just sit there, by the way; they move about within the nucleus at the rate of 40,000 miles per second.)

This discovery was cause for rejoicing among the "life is not solid but merely appears solid" school of believers. Not only was the empty space *between* atoms known to be large, but the space *within* atoms themselves—the space in which there was nothing at all—was many, many, *many* times greater than the "hard stuff" of electrons, protons and neutrons.

Then life got even easier for the "life is energy" school, and much harder for the "life is hard" school. The hard stuff—the electrons, protons and neutrons—started, uh, coming apart. They didn't come apart, actually; they just weren't as solid as some scientists would have liked

*Since finding out what
something is is largely a
matter of discovering
what it is like,
the most impressive
contribution to the growth
of intelligibility has been
made by the application
of suggestive metaphors.*

JONATHAN MILLER

to believe. It seems that protons and neutrons are not solid things in themselves, but are made up of *sub*atomic particles.

Then all hell broke loose in the "hard" camp, and all heaven broke loose among the believers. It was discovered that the subatomic particles might not be particles after all, but *waves*. Yes, waves. Waves of energy. Nothing solid at all. Anywhere.

And so the fundamental question facing physics is: are subatomic particles solid particles, or are they just waves (vibrations) we perceive as particles because our current machinery isn't sophisticated enough to perceive the vibrations yet?

In some experiments, the basic unit of life behaved as a particle. In precisely the same experiments, the basic unit of life behaved as a wave. The only difference, it was found, *was the scientist performing the experiment*.

In other words, to some scientists performing an experiment, life was little particles; other scientists, performing the same experiment, found that life was a wave. This shattered the centuries-old scientific principle of experiments producing precisely the same results no matter who performed the experiment.

Physicist Fritjof Capra, in the landmark book *The Tao of Physics*, described it this way:

> As we penetrate into matter, nature does not show us any isolated "basic building blocks," but rather appears as a complicated web of relations between the various parts of the whole. These relations always include the observer in an essential way. The human observer constitutes the final link in the chain of the observational processes, and the properties of any atomic object can be understood only in terms of the object's interaction with the observer.

Capra concludes, "In atomic physics, we can never speak about nature without, at the same time, speaking of ourselves."

*Some problems are just
too complicated for
rational, logical solutions.
They admit of insights,
not answers.*

JEROME WIESNER

*The scientific theory I like best is
that the rings of Saturn
are composed entirely
of lost airline luggage.*

MARK RUSSELL

Some have characterized the interaction between scientist and the particle/wave mystery in this way: What the scientist performing the experiment *expected* to find, the scientist found. If the scientist expected to find a wave, a wave was found. If the scientist expected to find a particle, a particle was found.

So the jury is out on the wave vs. particle controversy. But even if it turns out that subatomic particles are little bits of solid stuff, it's undeniably true that there are more spaces within supposedly solid things than solids. No less an authority than the *Encyclopædia Britannica* tells us, "An atom (and thus all matter) is mostly empty space."

This doesn't fit with our perception of—or even belief about—things at all. As *Britannica* tells us, "Some daily life concepts are no longer valid on the atomic scale."

For example, there is more empty space in the book you're holding, than book. The electrons in the atoms of the book are moving so fast, they give the *illusion* of solid ink on solid paper.

It's not. It's just an illusion. If all the electrons would stop moving for even an instant, the book would not just crumble into dust, it would disappear. Poof.

Please remember, we're not talking metaphysical nonsense here. We're talking hard, scientific fact. What you're reading is vibrating energy, giving the illusion of being a book. Most of us can't see the vibration because our senses can't perceive vibrations of that speed.

The same is true of whatever you're sitting (or lying) on, everything in the room or vehicle you're currently in, and everything you've ever seen, touched, heard, tasted or smelled.

It is also, by the way, true of your own body.

Welcome to life.

*Any sufficiently
advanced technology
is indistinguishable
from magic.*

ARTHUR C. CLARKE

What Did That Last Chapter Mean, Anyway?

So what does a chapter on atomic physics have to do with a book on life? A few facts of life can be gleaned from the study of the atom:

1. There is more nothing than something, even in things that appear to have more something than nothing.

2. Everything is always in motion, even things that don't appear to have moved in millions of years.

3. The perception that things are solid and stationary is an illusion.

4. All life is energy "pretending" to be something.

5. This energy somehow responds to human interaction.

If, in the pages of this book, we suggest you try something you may have never tried before, and give a seemingly weird explanation for why it might work, know that our explanation might have more to do with atomic physics than with metaphysics.

Life, it turns out, is not a struggle; it's a wiggle.

The only good is knowledge
and the only evil
is ignorance.

SOCRATES

Are Human Beings Fundamentally Good or Fundamentally Evil?

Good.

That's our answer, anyway. Our proof? Well, we could quote philosophers, psychologists and poets, but then those who believe that humans are fundamentally evil can quote just as many philosophers, psychologists and poets—and their list of p, p and p would probably outnumber ours.

Our proof is a simple one, going directly to the source of human life: an infant.

When you look into an infant's eyes, what do you see? We've looked into quite a few, and we have yet to see fundamental evil radiating from a baby's eyes.

There seems to be a purity, a joy, a brightness, a splendor, a sparkle, a marvel, a happiness—you know: good.

And yet, if we are fundamentally good, why is it when we relax, and listen to our thoughts or feel our emotions or sense our bodies, we often find so much rubbish? Here's our explanation for that, in the form of a diagram.

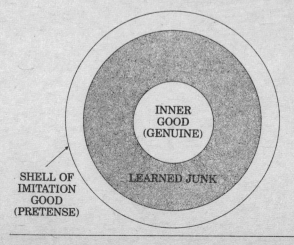

INNER GOOD (GENUINE)

LEARNED JUNK

SHELL OF IMITATION GOOD (PRETENSE)

*When choosing between
two evils, I always like
to try the one
I've never tried before.*

MAE WEST

Babies are like sponges; they absorb everything. By the time they are two years old, they have observed more than 10,000 hours of life: the good, the bad, the ugly—plus whatever was on TV.

As they begin to act out this array of observations, they are informed—sometimes in no uncertain terms—that some behavior is "good," some is "bad," and "around here" we don't do the bad, we only do the good.

What do we mean by "evil?" Evil is unnecessary life experience. Whatever we need to do to learn a lesson is life—even if it's "not fun." When the not-fun continues after the lesson is learned, that's evil. To cut off a dog's tail (when necessary) is life. To do it an inch at a time is evil.

At first, the child has trouble understanding why some things are "right" while others are "wrong." (This stage is referred to by some child-rearing manuals as The Terrible Twos.) But eventually, the child learns—with varying degrees of success—to cover the bad with the good, the wrong with the right.

The "evil" is learned by observing their environment, and the "good" is taught to them to hide that evil away. We are taught to pretend to be good, and when we let the pretense slip, we find evil lurking just below the surface. It's little wonder, then, that most people think their inner is bad. The struggle to keep up the "good act" is a "never ending battle for truth, justice, and the American Way."

When people have the patience (and courage) to go beneath the "inner evil," they find, invariably, a sea of peace, calm and joy. They have reached the inner good that is their true nature.

Ironically, this inner good is often remarkably similar to the "good shell" that was fabricated for them by the Parental Construction Company. The difference here is that, coming from this center, people do good because good is the thing to do, not because they're "supposed to" do good, or because they might get punished if they don't.

Your friends may think you're, say, a happy person. You might think, "What do they know? If only they knew how unhappy I am inside. I only pretend to be happy, and they fall for it. What kind of friends are these?" The truth

*Good people are good
because they've come to
wisdom through failure.*

WILLIAM SAROYAN

may be that beneath the unhappiness is a genuine happiness—and perhaps the happiness your friends see is the genuine happiness, not the pretense of happiness you use as a cover. Maybe your friends could see the genuine happiness all along.

This is true of any "good" emotion, thought or behavior: love, joy, gratitude, enthusiasm, compassion, generosity, tenderness, bravery, cleanliness, reverence and all the rest.

We'll have more on how to discover that wellspring of inner goodness within yourself (that is, by the way, one of the primary goals of this book). For now, please consider this: If you think you're fooling people with your act of goodness, and you think you aren't all that good, maybe the one you're fooling is yourself.

*Be wiser than other people,
if you can, but do not
tell them so.*

LORD CHESTERFIELD

PART TWO

ADVANCED TOOLS FOR
EAGER LEARNERS

Life is, if nothing else, a persistent teacher. It will repeat a lesson over and over (and over and over) until it is learned. How does life know we've learned? When we change our behavior (either inner, outer or both). Until then, even if we intellectually "know" something, we haven't really *learned* it. School remains in session.

The good news is that we learn all we need to know—eventually. The bad news: the lessons continue until they are learned.

For some, however, eventually is not soon enough. If there's something they can learn that will *eventually* make their lives happier, healthier and more productive, why not learn it *now?* That brings happiness, health and productivity to us sooner—and it avoids a lot of (perhaps painful) lessons along the way. That makes sense to us.

Others aren't content with learning only what they "need" to know. "Getting by" is not enough. They want more. They, like us, are the "eager learners" who read books with titles such as *LIFE 101.*

Someone once said that the only two things that motivate an enlightened person are love and curiosity. We can't speak for our state of enlightenment, but we can say that, considering our level of curiosity, it's a good thing we're not cats.

As Anatole France pointed out more than a hundred years ago, "The whole art of teaching is only the art of

*What a wonderful
day we've had.
You have learned
something, and I have
learned something.
Too bad we didn't
learn it sooner.
We could have
gone to the movies instead.*

BALKI BARTOKOMOUS
PERFECT STRANGERS

awakening the natural curiosity of young minds for the purpose of satisfying it afterwards."

But what if we're curious about things that seemingly can't be answered? When faced with this quandary, we like to comfort ourselves with the thoughts of Emerson: "Undoubtedly we have no questions to ask which are unanswerable. We must trust the perfection of the creation so far as to believe that whatever curiosity the order of things has awakened in our minds, the order of things can satisfy."

"Life was meant to be lived," Eleanor Roosevelt wrote in her autobiography, "And curiosity must be kept alive. One must never, for whatever reason, turn his back on life."

This section of the book has in it a series of tools designed to keep curiosity alive and thriving. These same tools can be used to find satisfying answers to the things you may be curious about. They are techniques designed to accelerate the process of learning.

All of these tools, by the way, are optional. No one *needs* to know or use any of them to learn the necessary lessons of life. As such, there's no need to struggle, thinking that if you don't master them your life will be a failure. Be easy with these techniques. Experiment. Play with them. Have fun.

At the same time, there's no need to teach these tools to anyone else—much less *insist* that people relate to you as though they've already mastered them. These skills are electives in the school of life. If you elect to use any or all of them for *your* accelerated learning, that's fine; but please don't expect—and certainly don't demand—that others accelerate their learning too.

Before we start, let's take a look at why human beings spend so much time struggling *against* learning; why we, as a species, seem so opposed to the exploration of new things.

Haven't you been curious about that?

*The only reason I always
try to meet and know the
parents better is because it
helps me to forgive
their children.*

LOUIS JOHANNOT

Why Do We Resist Learning?

If we're here to learn, and if we have this seemingly in-built desire to learn (curiosity), why do we resist learning so much? The classic example is the argument that goes, "Listen to me!" "No, you listen to me!" "No, you listen to me!" Et cetera.

It seems that somewhere around the age of eighteen (give or take ten years), something in us decides, "That's it, I've had it, I'm done. I know all I need to know and I'm not learning any more."

Why?

Let's return to the idea of the small child being taught about life by its parents. Parents are as gods to little children—the source of food, protection, comfort, love.

Also, parents are BIG! They're four to five times bigger than children. Imagine how much respect (awe? fear?) you'd have for someone twenty to thirty feet tall, weighing 800 to 1,000 pounds.

Let's imagine a child—two, three—playing in a room. The parents are reading, the child is playing, all is well. After an hour or so, CRASH! The child bumps a table and knocks over a lamp.

Where there once was almost no interaction with the parents, suddenly there is a lot—almost all of it negative. "How many times have we told you..." "Can't you do anything right?" "What's the matter with you?" "That was my favorite lamp!" Shame, bad, nasty, no good. This verbal tirade might or might not be reinforced by physical punishment.

What does the child remember from an evening at home with the folks? Does the child remember the hours spent successfully (i.e.: no broken anything) playing while mommy and daddy read, or does the child remember the intense ten minutes of "bad boy," "nasty girl," "shame, shame, shame," after the fall?

The negative, of course. It was loud and it was frightening (imagine a pair of twenty-to-thirty-foot, 1,000-

*I have found the best way to
give advice to your children
is to find out
what they want and then
advise them to do it.*

HARRY S TRUMAN

pound gods yelling at you). It was, for the most part, the *only* interaction the child may have had with "the gods" all evening. (Especially if being put to bed early is part of the punishment.)

When a child's primary memory of the communication from its parents ("the gods") is no, don't, stop that, shouldn't, mustn't, shame, bad, bad, bad, what is the child being taught about itself? That it can do no good; that it must be alert for failure at every moment, and still it will fail; that it is a disappointment, a letdown, a failure.

In short, a child begins to believe that he or she is fundamentally not good enough, destined for failure, and in the way. In a word, unworthy.

And there is very little in the traditional educational system to counteract this mistaken belief. If anything, school etches the image even deeper. (If we learned all we needed to know in kindergarten, it was promptly drummed out of us in first grade.) You are taught you must perform, keep up, and "make the grade," or you aren't worth much. If you *do* work hard at making the grades, some authority figure is bound to ask, "Why are you studying all the time? Why aren't you out playing with the other children? What's wrong with you? Don't you have any friends?"

Catch-22 never had it so good.

Naturally, we can't go around feeling unworthy *all the time*. It hurts too much. So we invent defenses—behaviors that give the *illusion* of safety. Soon we notice that others have not only adopted similar defenses, but have taken their defenses to new and exotic levels. The school of limitation is in session.

We begin hanging out with other members of the same club. We are no longer alone. In fact, we start to feel worthy. We have comrades, companions, cohorts, compatriots, confidants, confreres, counterparts and chums.

The clubs? There are basically four main chapters of the Let's Hide Away From All the Hurtful Unworthiness Clubs International. They are:

*I was thrown out of college
for cheating on the
metaphysics exam;
I looked into the soul
of the boy next to me.*

WOODY ALLEN

The Rebels

The rebels like to think of themselves as "independent." They have, in fact, merely adopted a knee-jerk reaction to whatever "law" is set before them. They are prime candidates for reverse psychology. ("The best way to keep children from putting beans in their ears is to tell them they *must* put beans in their ears.") They conform to nonconformity.

MOST FEARED FORTUNE COOKIE: "A youth should be respectful to his elders."

SLOGAN: "Authority, you tell us that we're no good. Well, authority, *you're* no good."

MOTTO (minus the first two words): "...and the horse you came in on!"

If the ones who tell you you're no good are no good, then, somehow, that makes you good. Somehow.

The Unconscious

These are the people who appear not all there because, for the most part, they're not all there. They're not dumb; they're just someplace else: a desert island, a rock concert, an ice cream parlor. They are masters of imagination. They are not stupid. They do their best, however, to *appear* dumb, drugged or asleep to anyone they don't want to deal with. They want, simply, to be left alone by all authority figures.

FAVORITE FORTUNE COOKIE: "To know that you do not know is the best."

SLOGAN: "You can't expect much from me, so you can't criticize me because, uh, um, what was I saying?"

MOTTO: "Huh?"

The real world picks them apart, so they retreat to a fantasy world of which they can be a part.

I'm an experienced woman;
I've been around...
Well, all right, I might
not've been around,
but I've been...nearby.

MARY RICHARDS
THE MARY TYLER MOORE SHOW

The Comfort Junkies

These are the ones who hide in comfort. All that is (or might be) uncomfortable is avoided (unless avoiding it would be more uncomfortable), and all that might bring comfort (food, distractions, TV, portable tape players, drink, drugs) is sought after (unless the seeking after them would be uncomfortable).

MOST FEARED FORTUNE COOKIE: "The scholar who cherishes the love of comfort is not fit to be deemed a scholar."

SLOGAN: "Comfort at any cost! (Unless it's too expensive.)"

MOTTO (taken from Tolkien): "In a hole in the ground there lived a hobbit. Not a nasty, dirty, wet hole, filled with the ends of worms and an oozy smell, nor yet a dry, bare, sandy hole with nothing in it to sit down on or to eat: it was a hobbit-hole, and that means comfort."

They memorize as much of their motto as is comfortable.

The Approval Seekers

The best way to prove worthiness is to have lots of people telling you how wonderful you are. These people work so hard for other people's approval (preferably) and acceptance (at the very least), they have little or no time to seek their own. But their own doesn't matter. They, after all, are unworthy, and what's the worth of an unworthy person's opinion? These people take the opposite tack of the rebels: rebels deem the opinions of others unworthy; acceptance seekers deem others' opinions *too* worthy. They would run for class president, but they're afraid of a backlash, so they usually win treasurer by a landslide.

MOST FEARED FORTUNE COOKIE: "Fine words and an insinuating appearance are seldom associated with true virtue."

SLOGAN: "What can I do for *you* today?"

MOTTO: "Nice sweater!"

Without such people, homecoming floats would never get built.

*A boy becomes an adult
three years before his
parents think he does,
and about two years after
he thinks he does.*

LEWIS B. HERSHEY

You've probably been able to place all your friends in their respective clubhouses. If you're having trouble placing yourself, you might ask a few friends. If their opinions tend to agree, you'll have your answer. You may not like it, but you'll have your answer.

(NOTE: If you reject the idea that you could possibly fit into any category, you're probably a rebel. If you accept your friend's evaluations too readily, you may be looking for approval. If you forget to ask, maybe you're unconscious. If you're afraid to ask, you may be seeking comfort. If a friend says, "You don't fit in any of these; you seem to transcend them all," that person is probably looking for *your* approval.)

Most of us tend to pay some dues to each club at one time or another, about one thing or another. We may, for example, be rebels when it comes to speed limits, unconscious when it comes to income tax, comfort-junkies when it comes to our favorite bad habit, and acceptance-seekers in intimate relationships.

These are also the four major ways people avoid learning. The rebels don't need to learn; the unconscious don't remember why they should; the comfortable find it too risky; and the acceptance-seekers don't want to rock any boats. ("Leave well enough alone.") Most of us have our own personal combination of the four—a little of this and a little of that—that have perhaps kept us from learning all we'd like to know.

How to surmount these ancient barriers? Tools, techniques, and practice, practice, practice. Where do we find these tools? The rest of this book is an encyclopedia of them.

Rule #1:
*Don't sweat
the small stuff.*

Rule #2:
It's all small stuff.

DR. MICHAEL MANTELL

Rules as Tools

One of the most effective tools for eager learners is one of the oldest—and one of the first to be resisted—rules.

As soon as we were able—as late as two for late-bloomers—we learned how to get around rules. The rebels rebelled, the unconscious forgot, the comfortable couldn't be bothered, and the approval-seekers slavishly obeyed—providing, of course, somebody was looking.

In most cases, rules were treated as the *enemy*, something laid out by an impersonal (and perhaps tyrannical) world, designed to limit us, punish us or upset us.

It's easy to see how rules could be thought of as the enemy. From a child's point of view, if there were no rules, our parents would never have been upset with us. Only when a rule was violated did they withdraw their love, and if those rules weren't there, then our parents would always love us. Or so goes the logic of a child.

Further, it seemed as though rules were some sort of childhood curse, like chicken pox, mumps or measles. Adults got to stay up late and watch TV. Adults got to eat two desserts if they wanted. Adults got to cross the street. Adults never had to take afternoon naps. "When *can* I do this?" we would ask. "When you're older," we were told.

Rules, we figured, were some temporary interference—like strained spinach or siblings—we had to endure and, one fine day, it would all be over. Imagine our surprise as we grew older—three, four, five—when we found that the number and complexity of rules actually *increased*.

Then came that repository of rules itself: school. After the initial shock, we gulped and, to one degree or another, accepted our fate: The rules will continue, unabated, for twelve more years. *Then* they will be over.

Hardly. What happened to many of the childhood rules was that we internalized them—they didn't go away, they just became a habit. We didn't play in traffic, not because it was a rule, but because we knew the conse-

Exit according to rule,
first leg and then head.
Remove high heels and synthetic
stockings before evacuation:
Open the door, take out the
recovery line and throw it away.

RUMANIAN NATIONAL AIRLINES
EMERGENCY INSTRUCTIONS

Is forbidden to
steal towels, please.
If you are not person to do such
is please not to read notice.

SIGN IN TOKYO HOTEL

quences of playing in traffic. We didn't stay up all night watching TV because we knew how we'd feel in the morning. We didn't have two desserts because—well, maybe we did. But we knew what it would do, and it did.

The confusion about rules when we were young was that some of the rules were useful to us, and some were not. We were, however, expected to follow *all* of them *or else*. The ones we found useful were no longer rules; they became a part of us. The ones that didn't become a part of us were "rules," and we hated them (or forgot about them, or ignored them, or followed them for approval—or some combination of these).

Take walking, for example. Walking is full of rules. Considering the size of our feet and the height of our body, human beings have no business standing at all. Try to get a Barbie doll (or G.I. Joe) to stand up without outside support—especially in heels. (G.I. Joe has a *very* difficult time in heels.)

If we forget any of the rules of walking, gravity exacts its "punishment." It is swift, unerring and constant. So we learn the rules of walking, and we make those rules our own.

We may not think of them as rules, but they are rules nonetheless. The same is true of talking, language, use of our hands, general body coordination, and so on. All the things we weren't born doing, we had to learn. Each has its own set of rules. Once we mastered the rules—made them our own—we forgot the rules and just did it.

Some rules are absolute, some arbitrary. "Keep breathing," is an absolute rule. "Drive on the right side of the road in North America," is an arbitrary rule. There's no special *reason* to drive on the right side of the road; approximately half the world drives on the left. It was conceived long ago by people we never knew. The reason it's a "good" rule is that, as long as everybody follows it, it works. We don't have to decide every time we pass an oncoming car which way to pass it. It saves time, attention, worry and—not insignificantly—lives.

Sometimes rule-following is part of "paying your dues." You may know a better way of doing things—that is, you may have a "new rule" that's better than the old

Robin: *Batgirl!*
What took you so long?

Batgirl: *You wouldn't*
believe the traffic,
and the lights were
all against me.
Besides, you wouldn't want
me to speed, would you?

Robin: *Your good driving*
habits almost cost us
our lives!

Batman: *No, Robin,*
she's right.
Rules are rules.

one—but in order to implement the improved rule, you have to follow the old rule for a while. In fact, once you master the old rule, you are then the master—and masters get to change things. Once you're successful at something, to do it another way is considered innovative. If you've yet to master the old way, it's often seen as rebellion.

We're certainly not saying "Conform and you'll be happy." (To be happy all the time is one of the most nonconformist things you can do, by the way. To be always joyful is not just rebellion, it's *radical*.) To change rules that are already in place takes time, energy, perseverance and a lot of hard work. You only have so many of these assets at your disposal, so choose with care the rules you want to change.

What we're suggesting is that you change your *view* of rules. This book is chock full of things you might see as "rules." If you treat them the way many people treat rules—with rebellion, unconsciousness, discomfort or as new ways to gain others' acceptance—these techniques will probably not be very useful. They'll just be more "should's," "must's," "ought-to's," and "have-to's." If you're like us, you already have plenty of those.

As we mentioned before, we're suggesting that you take each suggestion as a suggestion, try it out, see if it works for you, and if it does, use it. Then it's a tool, not a rule. If it doesn't work for you, let it go and move on to something that does. Then it's not a rule, it's just a tool that, for whatever reason, you have no use for at this time.

Here are three "rules" we have found to be the foundation for all the other rules we have adopted for ourselves. If "rules" is too strong a word, consider them perhaps *guidelines*. They've worked for us in every situation in which we've tested them. If you try them and they work for you, then they're your rules—tools—not ours. They're simple, but we've found that the challenges within them never seem to end.

*The ideas I stand
for are not mine.
I borrowed them
from Socrates.
I swiped them
from Chesterfield.
I stole them from Jesus.
And I put them in a book.
If you don't like their rules,
whose would you use?*

DALE CARNEGIE

1. Don't hurt yourself and don't hurt others. This begins at the physical level: don't hit people; don't steal from them; don't hit yourself in the head with a hammer. These are fairly easy to define. Then it moves to a more subtle level: don't put things in your body you know are not good for you; keep your body away from situations you know aren't good for it, etc.

It continues onto mental and emotional levels: don't judge yourself or others; knock off the guilts and resentments. Here we discover the "never-ending" part of the challenge: there always seems to be some subtler level at which we can stop doing harm to ourselves and to others.

2. Take care of yourself so you may help take care of others. Physically: get enough (but not too much) food, enough water, enough exercise, enough rest. Mentally and emotionally: praise yourself for work well done; enjoy each moment; love yourself. Again, easy to say, but it may take a lifetime of dedicated practice to achieve.

The second part of it, "so you may help take care of others," does not say you *must* help take care of others. It simply states the requirement ("take care of yourself") necessary for helping to take care of others *should you feel so inclined.* If you're not taking care of yourself first, you won't be able to help take care of others. If you *really* don't take care of yourself, others will be helping to take care of you.

3. Use everything for your upliftment, learning and growth. Everything. Everything. *Everything.* No matter what you do, no matter how stupid, dumb or damaging you judge it to be, there is a lesson to be learned from it. No matter what happens to you, no matter how unfair, inequitable or wrong, there's something you can take from the situation and use for your advancement.

We're not saying *intentionally* do silly things so you can learn, or *solicit* the evil of the world so you can gain something from it. No. We all do enough silly things, and the world does enough nastiness unto us, without our having to create or invite more. When you, naturally and without prompting, do these things—or they happen to you—*then* start looking for what you can do to lift, learn

*Pick battles
big enough to matter,
small enough to win.*

JONATHAN KOZOL

and grow. Remember the Writer's Creed: When the world gives you lemons, write *The Lemon Cookbook*.

There. Those three should keep you busy for, oh, the remainder of this life. Explaining the many facets of these rules—and ways you can grow from them—will take us (at least) the remainder of this book.

Let us, then, be up and doing,
With a heart for any fate;
Still achieving, still pursuing,
Learn to labor and to wait.

HENRY WADSWORTH LONGFELLOW
1839

Look, I really don't want to wax
philosophic, but I will say that if
you're alive, you got to flap your
arms and legs, you got to jump
around a lot, you got to make a
lot of noise, because life is the very
opposite of death. And therefore,
as I see it, if you're quiet, you're
not living. You've got to be noisy,
or at least your thoughts should
be noisy and colorful and lively.

MEL BROOKS

Participation

One of the greatest—and simplest—tools for learning more and growing more is *doing* more. It may or may not involve more activity. We're not talking, necessarily, about action but of *involvement*.

When we're involved, we learn more. If you want to learn more, become an eager participator. Take part. Involve yourself. Plunge in. Embrace new experiences. Partake of your own life.

It's hard to recommend specific activities; what truly engages one person might be mere amusement to another. The cliché, of course, is to recommend taking a walk over watching television. But with the video revolution—122 channels of cable, video rentals, and all the rest—television can now be as involving as anything else.

It's not so much *what* you do, but how you *respond* to what you do. Does the activity involve you in an active way? Does it engage your mind, body and emotions? (The full engagement of any *one* of these is participation—but learn to exercise the ones you tend to use less often.) Does it challenge you? Does it make you want to do more? If so, you're participating.

"Experimentation is an active science," Claude Bernard pointed out. Experiment. Make your life an active science.

*The last of
the human freedoms—
to choose one's attitude
in any given
set of circumstances,
to choose one's own way.*

VIKTOR FRANKL

Taking Charge

There's a lot of talk in personal growth circles about "taking charge." Everywhere we go, we hear people exclaiming: "I'm going to take charge of that!" "Why aren't you taking charge of this?" "I'm taking charge of my life!"

Taking charge is great, but many people misunderstand what it is, exactly, they can take charge of.

As far as we can tell, the only thing you can take charge of is *the space within the skin of your own body.* That's it. Everything (and, especially, everyone) else does not belong to that of which you can take charge.

Considering the vastness of the Universe, "the space within the skin of your own body" doesn't sound like much. But consider what's contained in there: your mind, your body, your emotions, and whatever sense of You you've got. That, to paraphrase Sir Thomas More, is not a bad public.

Even if we *could* take charge of people, things and events outside ourselves, our first job would *still* be to take charge of ourselves.

What would "taking charge" of yourself be like?

You would have charge of your thoughts. You would never find yourself thinking about things you didn't want to think about. Your mental focus would be directed, creative and positive at all times.

You would have charge of your body. You would be healthy, energetic, fit, glowing, radiant, exuberant and fully alive.

You would have charge of your emotions. You would never feel anything you didn't want to feel. You would feel joy, happiness, fulfillment, contentment, enthusiasm and love whenever you wanted to.

To the degree we do not have charge of our minds, bodies and emotions, we have our work cut out for us. Do we really have any *extra* time to spend taking charge of *others?*

Computers are useless.
They can only
give you answers.

PABLO PICASSO

Open the Mind, Strengthen the Body, Fortify the Emotions

We often let one of The Big Three run the show. What we said earlier of the mind is equally true of the body and emotions—they make great servants, but terrible masters.

You probably already know with which of The Big Three you tend to identify most closely; the one you give most influence, the one that most often "leads you into temptation," the one that stops you from doing the things you really want to do—or know it would be best for you to do.

If you let *you* run the show, you'll probably learn more, and, even if you don't, the show will be a lot more enjoyable. (Wouldn't *you* rather choose which videos *you* watch?) Sure, listen to the advice of the mind, body and emotions (more on this in Part Three, *Master Teachers in Disguise)*, but *you* make the decision, and move in the direction *you* choose. How? Here are some suggestions.

Open the Mind. We've probably all met lots of little Descartes running around, the ones who think therefore they are. (Remember Descartes? *"Cogito, ergo sum?"* We thought you'd remember.) You may have wanted to tell them, as Zorba told his "mental" young friend, "You think too much, that is your trouble. Clever people and grocers, they *weigh* everything."

These people spend a lot of time in opinions, evaluations, assessments, criticisms, judgments, convictions, laws, rules, procedures, schemes and making up their minds. Once their mind is made up, however, that's it; there's not much that can change it.

These are the people who worry most about brainwashing. Alas, they are also the ones whose brains may need a little washing.

To these folk, one and all, we simply suggest: the mind is like a parachute; it works best when open. The mental amongst us may protest, "California bumper sticker philosophy!" All right, how about this thought

You are a member
of the British royal family.
We are <u>never</u> tired, and we
all <u>love</u> hospitals.

QUEEN MARY

from Henry James: "Always keep a window in the attic open; not just cracked: open."

Strengthen the Body. If you're not doing what you want because you're "too tired," or you're worried that some person, germ or unlucky twist of fate is waiting to do you in, your body's probably got a hold of you.

Some people have a long list of physical reasons why they can't get things done: colds, flus, headaches, pulled this, sprained that, fractured something else. Is this what's troubling you, boobie?

Time to get hold of your body. Get up, get moving, get going. Your body is your vehicle, like your car. If you don't give your body direction, it's about as silly as letting your car choose its own direction. Get it out of the garage, step on the gas, get going.

It's your body: use it or lose it. Providing you give it sufficient rest, your body thrives on activity. Don't let your body stop you from doing what you want. Get up and do it anyway.

When you take the action of movement, the energy will be there—but not a second before. Don't wait for the energy before you do something; do and the energy will follow.

Fortify the Emotions. The overly emotional tend to wear their hearts of their sleeves. They act (or, more often, fail to act) because of what they feel. And what do they usually feel? Fear ("What if..."), guilt ("If I don't, then..."), anger, and disappointment ("Let down again. [sings] 'Alone again, naturally.'").

These people stay away from events in which their emotions *might* be aroused—particularly the emotions of fear, guilt, anger and disappointment ("hurt feelings"). They *fear* fear, guilt, anger and disappointment, so they stay away.

To these dear hearts we say: persevere. Press on. Feel the fear and do it anyway. Although the phrase "scared to death" is often used by the emotionals, very few people have actually died from fear. Emotions are not fragile. They are there to be used.

If you do not wish
to be prone to anger,
do not feed the habit;
give it nothing which
may tend to its increase.
At first, keep quiet and
count the days when
you were not angry:
"I used to be angry every
day, then every other day:
next, every two,
then every three days!"
and if you succeed in
passing thirty days,
sacrifice to the gods
in thanksgiving.

EPICTETUS

You strengthen your influence over your emotions by using them. Consciously put yourself in situations you want to avoid because of your feelings. Feel all there is to feel and, later, remind yourself that you survived.

After a while, you'll do more than survive: you'll thrive. Because the other side of fear is excitement. And the other side of doing is the reward and positive feelings you seek.

On the other hand, those who tend to be too often too angry at others need to exercise their feelings *less*. When we *don't* exercise something, it grows weaker. If you tend to lean toward resentment when things don't go your way, the next time you're peeved, try this: Rather than exercising your emotions, exercise your body. Run around the block. Do jumping jacks. Put on some music and dance. This may look silly to your friends and/or co-workers, but they'll probably prefer your taking a brief exercise break over the yelling, screaming, and/or pouting so often done by the easily ticked off.

(More on how to "take charge" of the mind, body and emotions later.)

≈

Did any of these sound too close for comfort? At some point or other, we all tend to be too mental, or too *un*-physical, or too emotional. If you've narrowed your specializations down to two and are having trouble choosing between them, maybe you have combined loyalties. This is not uncommon.

Some people, for example, have a combination of body and emotions. They add emotions to the usual lethargy of the body. These people are often hypochondriacs—and they have the symptoms to prove it.

Some combine the body with the mind. These people may belong to The Flat Earth Society. They don't do much, and they know precisely *why* they shouldn't. These people would do well to exercise more, both mentally and physically—work crossword puzzles while jogging, things like that.

*You're obviously suffering
from delusions of adequacy.*

ALEXIS CARRINGTON

Most common, it seems, are those who combine mind and emotions. When mind and emotions combine, it forms what is commonly referred to as "ego"—not necessarily by Freud's clinical definition, but by the more popular usage, as in, "He has an ego problem," or, "Her ego's out of control." The mind and emotions are a powerful combination. Learning to direct them only toward good—your own and others—is a challenge of epic proportions, of epic achievements, and of epic rewards.

(A great book on this subject is Dr. Albert Ellis' *How to Stubbornly Refuse to Make Yourself Miserable About Anything—Yes, Anything!* Available from: Institute for Rational-Emotive Therapy, 45 East 65th Street, New York, New York, 10021.)

*There are seasons, in human
affairs, when new depths
seem to be broken up in the soul,
when new wants are unfolded in
multitudes, and a new and
undefined good is thirsted for.
There are periods when to dare,
is the highest wisdom.*

WILLIAM ELLERY CHANNING
1829

*What we have to do is to be
forever curiously testing
new opinions and
courting new impressions.*

WALTER PATER
1873

Try New Things

The more we do, the more we learn. Even if we don't do it "right," we have at least learned yet another way of *not* doing it. That's learning; that's growth.

So, you don't (yet) know how to do something. So? "For the things we have to learn before we can do them, we learn by doing them." And that was said by none less than Aristotle.

We're not suggesting you do more of what you already find comfortable. We're encouraging you to explore the things you find *un*comfortable—the ones you're afraid to do, the ones you don't think you'd have the energy to do, the ones you're sure you'll be judged harshly by others if you do.

The underlying question in trying new things: Would I hurt myself *physically* (not emotionally, not mentally) if I did this? Not *could* (we *could* hurt ourselves doing almost anything), but *would*. If the answer is no, then do it.

It may not be comfortable (it's not supposed to be), and you may make a lot of mistakes (count on it), but you'll learn more than if you sat home in, "That indolent but agreeable condition of doing nothing," as Pliny (the Younger) put it a couple thousand years ago.

And that's the way it is.

WALTER CRONKITE

Acceptance

Acceptance is such an important commodity, some have called it "the first law of personal growth."

Acceptance is simply seeing something the way it is and saying, "That's the way it is."

Acceptance is not approval, consent, permission, authorization, sanction, concurrence, agreement, compliance, sympathy, endorsement, confirmation, support, ratification, assistance, advocating, backing, maintaining, authenticating, reinforcing, cultivating, encouraging, furthering, promoting, aiding, abetting or even *liking* what is.

Acceptance is saying, "It is what it is, and what is is what is." Great philosophers from Gertrude Stein ("A rose is a rose is a rose") to Popeye ("I am what I am") have understood acceptance.

Until we truly accept *everything*, we can not see clearly. We will always be looking through the filters of "must's," "should's," "ought-to's," "have-to's," and prejudices.

When reality confronts our notion of what reality *should* be, reality always wins. (Drop something while believing gravity *shouldn't* make it fall. It falls anyway.) We don't like this (that is, we have trouble *accepting* this), so we either struggle with reality and become upset, or turn away from it and become unconscious. If you find yourself upset or unconscious—or alternating between the two— about something, you might ask yourself, "What am I not accepting about this?"

Acceptance is not a state of passivity or inaction. We are not saying you can't change the world, right wrongs or replace evil with good. Acceptance is, in fact, the first step to successful action.

If you don't fully accept a situation precisely the way it is, you will have difficulty changing it. Moreover, if you don't fully accept the situation, you will never really know if the situation *should* be changed.

*Education is the ability to
listen to almost anything
without losing your temper
or your self-confidence.*

ROBERT FROST

When you accept, you relax; you let go; you become patient. This is an enjoyable (and effective) place for either participation or departure. To stay and struggle (even for fun things: how many times have you tried *real hard* to have a good time?), or to run away in disgust and/or fear is not the most fulfilling way to live. It is, however, the inevitable result of nonacceptance.

Take a few moments and consider a situation you are not happy with—not your greatest burden in life, just a simple event about which you feel peeved. Now accept *everything* about the situation. Let it be the way it is. Because, after all, it *is* that way, is it not? Also, if you accept it, you will feel better about it.

After accepting it, and everything about it, you probably still won't *like* it, but you may stop hating and/or fearing it. At worst, you will hate it or fear it a little less.

That's the true value of acceptance: you feel better about life, and about yourself. Everything we've said about acceptance applies to things you have done (or failed to do) as well. In fact, everything we've said about acceptance applies *especially* to your judgments of you.

All the things you think you should have done that you didn't do, and all the things you did that you think you shouldn't have done, accept them. You did (or didn't) do them. That's reality. That's what happened. No changing the past. You can struggle with the past, or pretend it didn't happen, or you can accept it. We suggest the latter. A life of guilt, fear and unconsciousness is, to say the least, not much fun.

Even a prime-time disciplinarian such as St. Paul admitted, "That that I should do I don't do, and that that I do I should not." And *that* was a man who knew his should's! The next time you find yourself doing something you "shouldn't," or not doing something you "should," you might as well accept it. "If it was good enough for St. Paul, it's good enough for me."

While you're at it, you might as well accept all your future transgressions against the "should's," "must's," and "have-to's" of this world. You will transgress. Not that we necessarily *endorse* transgression. We do, however, accept the fact that human beings do *do* such things, and if you

*When you make a mistake,
admit it. If you don't, you only
make matters worse.*

WARD CLEAVER

*No matter how cynical you get,
it is impossible to keep up.*

LILY TOMLIN

haven't yet accepted your humanity—with all the magnificence and folly inherent in that—now might be a good time to start.

When you're in a state of nonacceptance, it's difficult to learn. A clenched fist cannot receive a gift, and a clenched psyche—grasped tightly against the reality of what *must not be* accepted—cannot easily receive a lesson.

Relax. Accept what's already taken place—whether done by you or something outside of you. Then look for the lesson. You might not enjoy everything that happens in life, but you can enjoy the fact that no matter what happens, "there's a lesson in here someplace."

*I bid him look into
the lives of men
as though into a mirror,
and from others to take
an example for himself.*

TERENCE

190-159 B.C.

The Mirror

Whenever we look outside ourselves, we tend to evaluate. (Actually, we tend to judge, but the word evaluate is a softer one with which to begin a chapter.) Those evaluations tell us about the people and things around us.

But what if those evaluations also tell us valuable information about *ourselves?* That's the concept of "the mirror."

It goes like this: whatever we find "true" about the people and things around us, is also true about ourselves. When we evaluate anything outside ourselves, what we are doing is looking into a mirror; the mirror reflects back to us information about ourselves.

At first, this concept may seem rather far-fetched. Once you start using the concept, however, you may find it remarkable. You may not always *like* what you see in the mirror, you may not always be comfortable with it, but, if you want to learn about yourself more quickly (and that's what the techniques in this section of the book are designed to do), looking at yourself in the mirror of people and things is a valuable tool.

Remember the first time you heard your voice on a tape recorder, or saw yourself on videotape? "I don't sound like that!" "I don't behave that way!" Meanwhile, all your friends are saying, "Yes, that's what you sound like. Yes, that's precisely how you behave."

The first time *we* saw ourselves on videotape, we wondered how we had any friends at all. In time, with repeated viewings, we learned to accept the images of ourselves on the tape, and from that point of acceptance, we could begin making changes. (We like to think of them as *improvements.)*

And so it is with the mirror of life. You may not like all you see in the mirror, but until you look into the mirror and accept all that you see *about yourself*, you will not be able to make the changes (improvements) you'd like.

Let's say you look at someone and think, "They are angry, and I don't like that." Could it be you don't like it

*When we see men of a
contrary character,
we should turn inwards
and examine ourselves.*

CONFUCIUS

when you are angry? If you look at someone and say, "They're scared. I wish they'd just do it." Could there be something you're scared about; something you wish you would "just do"?

To evaluate and blame others does us little good. What do we learn? That we can evaluate and blame? We probably know we can do that just fine.

Using the mirror, we see that we judge and blame *ourselves*. Now, this is information we can do something about. We can, for example, stop judging and blaming ourselves, or at the very least accept the fact that we do judge and blame ourselves.

(Most people, when they discover they judge and blame themselves, begin to judge and blame the fact that they judge and blame themselves. When they notice that they are judging and blaming themselves for judging and blaming themselves, they begin to judge and blame themselves for *that*. It can become like the layers of an onion.)

Sometimes, we have to shift our focus a bit to see what it is about ourselves that's being reflected by others. For example, you may look at someone smoking and not like it. If we asked you to look in the mirror, you might say, "I don't smoke, how does that apply to me?"

What is it you don't like about the other person's smoking? "It's unhealthy." Then, the question is: What do *you* do that's not in the best interest of your health? "Smoking is inconsiderate." What do *you* do that's inconsiderate? "Smoking is a bad habit." What's your worst habit? "It's a waste of money." What do *you* waste money on? "It shows no self-control." Of what part of *your*self would you like to have more control?

Get the idea? There are other people's actions, and then there are the judgments we place upon those actions. If we move from the *action* we judge, and look at the *judgment*, we usually find a similar judgment we make about ourselves.

It's fun to extend this idea beyond people and include things as well. "This car never works when I want it to." What about you never works when you want it to? "It always rains at the worst possible time." What do you do

*It is no use to blame the
looking glass if your face is awry.*

NIKOLAI GOGOL
1836

*There is no human problem
which could not be solved
if people would simply
do as I advise.*

GORE VIDAL

at the worst possible time? "This steak is too tough." What about you could use a little tenderizing?

How does knowing this about yourself help? First, it gives you lots of material on which to practice acceptance. Can you accept everything you already know about yourself, and also everything you learn about yourself by looking into the mirror of other people's behavior? Your harshest judgments of others are the very ones you must accept about yourself. Can you do it? We know you can. *Will* you do it? Only you know the answer to that.

Second, the mirror also focuses you back on something (that is, *someone)* you *can* do something about. (Ever notice how little effect your judgments have had on others?) Which brings us to our first Pop Quiz. (Yes, *LIFE 101* has Pop Quizzes, just like school.)

To continually have "good advice" for a world that, for the most part, is completely disinterested in (and sometimes hostile to) advice of any kind:

(A) is a waste of time
(B) is a waste of good advice
(C) tends to alienate self from others
(D) tends to alienate others from self
(E) promotes self-righteousness in the giver
(F) promotes resentment in the receiver
(G) all of the above

Guess who could *really use* all that good advice? For the answer, we quote from Michael Jackson's song *Man in the Mirror*: "If you want to make the world a better place, take a look at yourself and make a change." All that good advice you've been giving to others (or would give to others if they only had the intelligence to ask) *finally* has a home. You.

And, as you're the only one you can really change, the only one who can really use all your good advice is yourself. Isn't it wonderful that the *advice giver* and the *best user* of the advice are the same person? (NOTE: If you're thinking, "I have to tell so-and-so this. They need to take some more of their own advice," remember the mirror. It's probably *you* who needs to take more of *your own* advice.)

Why do you look at
the speck of sawdust
in your brother's eye
and pay no attention to
the plank in your own eye?
How can you say
to your brother,
"Let me take the speck out
of your eye," when all the
time there is a plank
in your own eye?
You hypocrite,
first take the plank
out of your own eye,
and then you will
see clearly to remove the
speck from your
brother's eye.

MATTHEW 7:3-5

Again, sometimes we must shift the focus and ask ourselves the larger question in order to see how the advice we give another would fit ourselves.

If your advice to so-and-so is to be more careful with his money, and you don't think you need that advice because you already are careful with your money, what *do* you need to be more careful about? If your advice to thus-and-such is to exercise more, and you already exercise a lot, what part of yourself (other than your body) could do with a bit more exercise?

When we look into the mirror of life and see all there is within ourselves that needs, shall we say, improvement, we know we're going to be at it for some time: changing what we can, doing our best with what we can't, accepting and forgiving it all—whenever we remember to do so. (We know, for example, that we're really writing this book for ourselves, and if you care to look over our shoulders as we learn from our own "good advice," you are most welcome.)

We also see that whenever we lash out at another, we are really lashing out at ourselves. In this context, to strike another is as silly as striking the bathroom mirror because it's giving you a reflection you don't like. We can only pray that in our striking out, we don't hurt the mirror—especially when that mirror is another person. Could that be where the superstition, "If you break a mirror, it's seven years bad luck," comes from?

Thus far, we've only been talking about the "glass darkly" side of the mirror concept. It does have a lighter side. Bathroom mirrors also reflect what's good about us. And so, too, does the mirror of life.

All the people and things that you find loving, affectionate, caring, devoted, tender, wonderful, compassionate, beautiful, adorable, magnificent and sacred are simply mirroring to you the loving, affectionate, caring, devoted, tender, wonderful, compassionate, beautiful, adorable, magnificent and sacred parts of yourself.

The lighter side of the mirror concept is sometimes more difficult for people to accept than the darker side. "I can see that I'm impatient when I judge someone else for being impatient," you may say, "but when I see the

*Mirrors should reflect a little
before throwing back images.*

JEAN COCTEAU

*Honest criticism is hard to take,
particularly from a relative,
a friend, an acquaintance,
or a stranger.*

FRANKLIN P. JONES

majesty of a mountain, what does that have to do with me?" Everything. That purple mountain majesty is in you, too.

In fact, it's not really in the mountain at all. What's in the mountain is rock. What we, as humans, *project onto* the mountain is majesty. That's one of the reasons the mirror concept works. Most of the time we are projecting *something* onto almost *everything*. When the projection returns to us, we can see it as a reflection—which it is—or we can pretend it is emanating from the thing we projected the reflection onto.

The illusion that what we projected is coming from the thing we projected it onto is a deceptive one. We tend to get lost in the illusion, just as we tend to get lost in the illusion of the images projected on a movie screen. It is, nonetheless, an illusion, and the source of the projection at the movie theater is the projector. The source of the things we think and feel about others, is ourselves.

Using the mirror concept, we can begin to recognize the true source of the projections we send out. We begin to see that this person wasn't so bad after all. It was, in fact, what we were projecting onto them. We see that this other person wasn't so wonderful after all. We were merely projecting our own wonderfulness upon them.

The more you use it, the more you will probably find the mirror concept works. Please remember, this is an advanced tool for learning. There is, however, an *advanced* advanced version of this. It's called relationships.

The best mirror
is an old friend.

GEORGE HERBERT
1651

Relationships

Most people seek relationships to *get away from themselves*. But not eager learners! We use everything for our upliftment, learning and growth—including relationships. One of the most important things we can learn from a relationship is what the relationship can teach us about ourselves.

Relationships can be among the most amazing mirrors around. Some relationships are like fun-house mirrors: they reflect something back to you, but it's liable to be distorted. Other relationships are like magnifying or reducing mirrors: they make everything they reflect seem larger or smaller than they truly are.

Some relationships are accurate mirrors of the darkness inside us, others accurately reflect the light. Occasionally, we find one that reflects both. That's the relationship we either flee from, or "grapple to our hearts with hoops of steel."

We're using the term relationship in the broadest possible sense. Relationships truly take place inside ourselves. We have a relationship with anyone or anything we encounter. Have you ever read a book by an author who has long since shucked this mortal coil, and still felt a relationship? Or felt close to a movie character, knowing all the while the character never even existed?

What we do inside ourselves about the people (and things) we choose to be in relationship with can be one of the greatest learning tools in the entire repertoire—especially when combined with the mirror.

The next time you think about someone, "I hate you," ask yourself, "What is it this person is reminding me about myself that I hate?" And the next time you think about another, "I love you," ask yourself, "What is it about myself I love that I see in this person, too?"

Answering—and accepting the answers to—these questions lays the foundation for not just personal learning, but for enjoyable, productive relationships with others.

What the inner voice says
Will not disappoint
the hoping soul.

SCHILLER
1797

I thank you for your voices,
thank you,
Your most sweet voices.

SHAKESPEARE

Inner Voices

It doesn't take much inner listening to know that "in there" there are many voices: speaking, singing, shouting, and whispering. At times, we're sure we have an entire tabernacle choir.

Some of the "voices" speak, others show images. Some communicate using feelings, while others communicate to us through a sense of "knowing." When we say "voices," we include all of these—and any other forms of communication we failed to mention.

These voices have information for you—all of it useful. Some you can use by following; some you can use by doing precisely the opposite. It's a matter of knowing whether or not a given voice is on your side.

How do you know? Listen. (Listen might not be the best word. *Perceive* might be a better word, or *look within,* or *be aware of* your inner process. We'll use listen, because it goes along with the analogy of "voices," but know that when we say "listen" we also mean watch, sense, perceive and be aware of what's going on inside.)

Start by listening and keeping track of which voice says what. You can assign them characters, if you like. Here are four of our inner favorites:

The critic. We see this voice as a vulture. Pick, pick, pick, nag, nag, nag. Nothing we, or anyone else, does is good enough. (Except occasionally when somebody does something undeniably outstanding, then the vulture says, "Well, *you'll* never do anything that good.") Doom and gloom fly with the vulture. It feeds on unworthiness, and its droppings are the doubts, fears and judgments that keep us from moving toward our goals.

The praiser. The praiser we see as an eagle. It proudly tells us all the wonderful things we are, have and do. It generously praises the beingness, accomplishments and activities of others. It's the one that lets us know we are worthy *no matter what,* and that our worth does not need to be proven, earned or defended. We are worthy just because we are. All that we are is fine just the way it

The voice of
the turtledove
speaks out. It says:
Day breaks,
which way are you going?

Lay off, little bird,
must you so scold me?
I found my lover on his bed,
and my heart was sweet to excess.

LOVE SONGS OF THE NEW KINGDOM
1550-1080 B.C.

I will neither yield to
the song of the siren nor
the voice of the hyena,
the tears of the crocodile
nor the howling of the wolf.

GEORGE CHAPMAN
1605

is. It flies on the wings of grace and gratitude. It nurtures our very beingness.

The dummy. The dummy is a turkey. It's the one who answers quickly and loudly, "I don't know," to almost any question. The turkey is the one that keeps us doing all those stupid things we do, and then says, "Darn! I knew better!" We may know better, but no one told the turkey. Turkeys do not fly. If you leave them out in the rain they will drown. They have nothing to be thankful for on Thanksgiving.

The knower. The knower is like an egg. An egg? Yes, as W. S. Gilbert said, "As innocent as a new-laid egg." That's one of the attributes of our knower—each moment is new, fresh and innocent. Or as Hans Christian Anderson pointed out, "His own image was no longer the reflection of a clumsy, dirty, gray bird, ugly and offensive. He himself was a swan! Being born in a duck yard does not matter, if only you are hatched from a swan's egg." Our knower knows who we are and the kind of bird in the egg, (HINT: It ain't no vulture). It has sufficient self-love to keep itself warm and cozy while gestating. It knows the hatching will take place at precisely the right moment. It is content and divinely patient until then. As Robert Burns wrote of his egg, "The voice of Nature loudly cries, / And many a message from the skies, / That something in us never dies."

It's a good idea to listen to *what* the voices say, not to *how* they say it. As Lord Byron reminds us, "The Devil hath not, / in all his quiver's choice, / An arrow for the heart like a sweet voice." And Freud, a century later, wrote, "The voice of the intellect is a soft one, but it does not rest until it has gained a hearing. Ultimately, after endlessly repeated rebuffs, it succeeds. This is one of the few points in which one may be optimistic about the future of mankind, but in itself it signifies not a little."

If all these birds in our brains are too much for you, perhaps you could use the metaphor of tuning a radio, or changing channels on a television. Once you tune into your own network of wisdom, you'll have guidance that's sure, clear and direct. (You may not always want to follow it, but you'll know it's there nonetheless.)

*More than any time
in history mankind
faces a crossroads.
One path leads to despair
and utter hopelessness,
the other to total extinction.
Let us pray that we have
the wisdom to choose
correctly.*

WOODY ALLEN

Accountability

To the degree the events of the world happen *to* us, we are powerless pawns in a game of chance. The most we can do is hope, have lots of insurance, and buy emergency food supplies.

To the degree we know that *we* have *something* to do with what happens to us, we gain authority, influence and control over our lives. We see that by changing our attitudes and actions, we can change what happens to us.

In a word, we become accountable.

When something happens to you, you can explore it and probably see that you had *something* to do with its taking place. You either created it, promoted it, or—at the very least—*allowed* it. (To remember the words create, promote and allow, just remember C.P.A. = accountant = accountability.)

When looking for areas of accountability, we suggest you not start with the biggest disaster of your life. Start with the daily slings and arrows that flesh is heir to. Looking for accountability is like exercise—don't try to run a marathon if you've been sedentary for twenty years.

Pick a simple "it happened to me" event—misplacing your keys, the plumber not showing up, running out of gas—and see how you *might* have had *something* to do with creating, promoting or allowing it to happen. Helpful hints:

1. Go back in time. We love to start our "victim stories" at the point they started happening to us—when the you-know-what hit the fan, and the fan was running. If you start at an earlier point, however, you see that you promised yourself to always put your keys in the same place and you failed to do so; the plumber was not known for his reliability; and the low-gas indicator light on your car had been on for so long you thought your car must be solar-powered.

2. What was I pretending not to know? What intuitive flashes did you ignore? "I'd better get some spare keys made," as you passed the hardware store a month

*Well, if you've got
work to do, Wallace,
I don't want to interfere.
I was reading an article in
the paper the other day
where a certain amount of
responsibility around
the home was good
character training.
Goodbye, Mr. and Mrs.
Cleaver.*

EDDIE HASKELL

ago? "This guy's not going to show," when you first spoke to the plumber? "I'd better get some gas," as you passed the 35th station since the gas indicator light came on? We all know a lot more than we pretend to know.

Into all this comes a perfectly good word that has been given a bad rap—responsibility. Responsibility simply means the *ability* to *respond*. Most people, however, use it to mean blame. "Who's responsible for this!" usually means "Who can I blame for this?"

In any situation, we have the ability to respond, and our response will make the situation either better or worse. Whichever way it goes, we have the ability to respond again. And again. And again. By exercising our ability to respond, and watching the results closely, we can, if we so choose, lift almost any situation.

One ability to respond we always have is how we react *inside* to what's going on *outside*. The world can be falling apart around us; that doesn't mean we have to fall apart inside. Remember: It's OK to feel good when things are going bad. (See the chapter *Taking Charge.*)

True accountability has three parts. First, acknowledge that you have *something* to do with what's happened. Even if you're not sure what that might be, ask yourself, *"If I did* create, promote or allow this, what might that be?"* The answer may surprise you.

Second, explore your response options. In other words, become response-able.

Third, take a corrective action. The more accountability you found at the first step, the more corrective action you may want to take here. On the other hand, your corrective action might be getting out of the way and letting those who are more accountable than you take care of things. To give an example: if you spilt the glass of milk, clean up the milk. If a milk truck spills milk all over the highway, get off the highway.

And remember: you create, promote or allow all the *good* things that happen to you, too.

*When an emotional injury
takes place, the body begins
a process as natural as the
healing of a physical wound.
Let the process happen.
Trust that nature
will do the healing.
Know that the pain will
pass and, when it passes,
you will be stronger,
happier, more sensitive and
aware.*

*HOW TO SURVIVE
THE LOSS OF A LOVE*

Good Mourning

This is a lifetime of good-byes. As we continue with life, we will say good-bye to cherished people, things and ideas. Eventually, we say good-bye to life itself with our death. Learn to say a good good-bye. Allow yourself to mourn each loss. As with a physical wound, the body has its own schedule for healing. It will tell you when it has healed.

Understanding the process of recovering from an emotional wound is valuable—not necessarily as a technique for accelerating the healing process—but more as an assurance that, no matter what stage of recovery you are in, all is well.

There are three distinct, yet overlapping, phases of recovery. We go through each phase no matter what the loss. The only difference is intensity of feeling, and duration. In a minor loss, we can experience all three stages in a few minutes. In a major loss, the recovery process can take years.

The first stage is **shock/denial.** Our body and emotions numb themselves to the pain. The mind denies the loss. Often, the first words we utter when hearing of a loss is "Oh, no," or "This can't be."

The second stage is **anger/depression**. We are angry at whatever or whomever caused the loss (including the person who left). We often turn the anger within and feel guilt over something we did or did not do. (This assignment of blame, either outer or inner, is not always rational.) The depression stage of recovery is the sadness often associated with loss: the tears, the hurt, the desolation. We fear that we will never love or be loved again.

The third stage is **understanding/acceptance**. We realize that life does go on, that loss is a part of life, and that our life can and will be complete without the presence of that which was lost. We also realize that, by going through the first two stages of recovery, we have learned a great deal about ourselves, and that we are a better person for the experience.

*In the darkest hour the soul is
replenished and given strength
to continue and endure.*

HEART WARRIOR CHOSA

God gave burdens, also shoulders.

YIDDISH PROVERB

If we don't allow ourselves the time and freedom to heal, some of our ability to experience life is frozen—locked away—and is unavailable for the "up" experiences we seem to like: happiness, contentment, love, peace. The mechanism that feels the anger and depression is the same one that feels peace and love. If you refuse to feel the anger and the pain of a loss, you will not be able to feel anything else until that area heals.

In the past, perhaps we denied the hurt of loss—through overwork, drugs (including alcohol and cigarettes), other addictive activities, or sheer force of will. ("I will *not* feel sad about this any more!") If this is true, there may be areas of past loss that remain unhealed.

When you open yourself to greater learning about yourself, these areas may "thaw," and the feelings of sadness, fear and anger may surface. If this happens, love yourself enough to go through the healing process you did not allow yourself earlier. You do not need to know what the loss was—it may be a combination of several losses over many years—you just need to let yourself heal this time. Give yourself the gift of healing.

In other words, stay out of your own way. Let yourself feel bad if you want to feel bad. Feel joy, too. Healing is taking place. An unavailable portion of yourself is now being reclaimed for future enjoyment.

Sometimes a current loss may trigger a previous, still unhealed loss. You may wonder, for example, "Why am I so upset by a rejection from this person? I just met him (or her)." It may be that the healing of a former relationship—one that meant a great deal more to you—is taking place.

How to heal? Use all the techniques in this book: most techniques for growth and learning are excellent for healing and recovery. You might want to read *How to Survive the Loss of a Love* (by Melba Colgrove, Ph.D. and Peter McWilliams. If you're interested in a copy, please call 1-800-LIFE-101).

The primary keys: use the light, love yourself, forgive yourself, everyone and everything involved (each of these will be discussed more fully in upcoming chapters), and accept what is.

*I don't want the cheese,
I just want to get out of
the trap.*

SPANISH PROVERB

Learn to Let Go

How does one avoid loss in the first place? Contrary to popular belief, it's not *attachment* that causes loss—attachment feels fine. It's *de*tachment that hurts. Learn to let go.

Some suggest that to avoid loss, one should never be attached to anything. They give the example of a hand in water: when the hand is removed from the water, the hand leaves no impression. These people say the reason the hand leaves no trace in the water is because the water is not attached to the hand.

On the contrary, while the hand is in the water, it is *very* attached to the hand. It surrounds it, enfolds it, embraces it. Allow yourself to experience life as fully as water experiences the hand, then let go as completely as water.

Yes, the water leaves a little of itself on the departing hand, as we leave a little of ourselves with the people and things we touch, but for the most part, when it comes time to go, let go.

The hand could no more hold the water than the water could hold the hand. As soon as one "wants" to leave, there is no attachment, because there *can be* no attachment other than the mutual action of being together. Hand and water both accept the inevitability, and part "clean."

There is a title for a book on raising children we've always liked, *Hold Them Very Close, and Let Them Go.* This we find good advice for all experiences, whatever they may be: Hold them very close, and let them go.

How do you know when it's time to hold them close? When they're in front of you (often literally): Whatever is the current experience in your awareness; the next event on your schedule. When is it time to let go? When you're on your way out or they're on their way out.

Say good-bye, let go, and embrace the new moment.

*You do not need
to leave your room.
Remain sitting at your table
and listen.
Do not even listen,
simply wait.
Do not even wait,
be quite still and solitary.
The world will freely
offer itself to you
to be unmasked,
it has no choice,
it will roll in ecstasy
at your feet.*

FRANZ KAFKA

Observation

Earlier, we talked about "taking charge" of the mind, body and emotions. "How do I do that?" you might have asked. One method is observation.

You could think of observation as a meditation of acceptance. You sit and simply accept *everything* that happens, both inner and outer. Consider: almost the only time you want to respond to something outside yourself is when something inside demands it.

What is that inner demand? What is the voice (or voices) that insist that you do this, or run away from that? Why do you sometimes follow that voice so automatically (maybe even unconsciously)? The answers to these questions are individual, and the answers lie in observation.

To observe, don't *do* anything, simply observe the inner process. The voices may rise to screaming crescendo. Don't do anything; continue to observe.

At first, observation is best practiced alone. Set a timer for a given length of time (start with, say, five minutes and build up). Sit in a comfortable position, close your eyes, and tell yourself, "I'm not going to move my body until the timer goes off." Then sit and observe.

The inner voices may start quietly, but as they feel "ignored," they tend to get louder. One may want you to shift your position. Don't. Observe the voice demanding that you shift. One may want you to scratch an itch. Don't. Observe the itch; observe the emotional reaction to not scratching the itch. ("It's my body, and I can scratch it if I want to!") Observe it all. If the phone rings, observe the desire to answer it. Don't answer it. Observe it. Observe your inner reaction to an outer ringing.

This may sound easy on paper. The inner voices that don't want to lose control often say at this point, "That would be no problem for us; we don't need to do that." Try it and see.

*If you resist evil,
as soon as it's gone,
you'll fold.*

KEN KESEY

As we increase the amount of time we observe while sitting still, we can then start observing while moving around.

Time for a Pop Quiz!

Observation shows us:

(A) our inner reactions to outer experiences;
(B) that it's our reaction to what happens around us, not what happens around us, that motivates us;
(C) the demands the voices inside us make;
(D) we don't have to do anything with, to or about the voices;
(E) we don't have to do anything about most outer experiences;
(F) all of the above.

Observation leads us to a point of neutrality—we don't *have to* react, either positively or negatively, to any situation. We simply have to be. Or, better, we simply *are.*

Neutrality is not neuter, nor is it like "Neutral" in a car. We *can* engage our gears and move ahead in neutral. In fact, when not reacting—almost-reflexively—to this, that and everything, our action becomes more effective. We can maintain an inner calm and still be dynamically involved.

Another way of viewing this: observation disconnects our buttons. We know that when someone "pushes our button," we react. Push, react. Push, react. Push, react. We are no longer in control; the person or thing pushing the button is.

Through observation, we notice that it's not the *pushing* of the button, but our *reaction* to the pushing of the button that causes our response. Eventually, by intentionally not responding and simply observing their pushing and our reacting, the push-react connection is dissolved. (We will discuss in Parts Four and Five ways of reconnecting the buttons to the responses *you* want.)

Think of "observing" as "obviously serving" yourself, and "neutral" as "new trails" of freedom, fun and adventure.

*I hear that you're building
Your house
deep in the desert.
Are you living for
nothing now?
I hope you're keeping
Some kind of record.*

LEONARD COHEN

Keep a Record of Your Progress

Record each day, in some way:

- The lessons you learn.
- The good that you do.
- The good that happens to you.
- The insights you have.
- Anything else that seems of interest.

The "classical" way of recording such things is, of course, a journal or a diary. ("Keep a diary, and someday your diary will keep you."—Mae West.) It need not, however, be that formal. You might have a box into which you toss mementos, letters, matchbook covers (etc.) and dated notes to yourself.

In this electronic age, you might keep a file in your computer. Using your word processor, you can include copies of your best letters, poems, etc. in your journal file, and include the best from your electronic journal in letters, manuscripts, and so on.

You could use a tape recorder and "debrief" yourself each evening, or take along a portable unit and record things "as they happen."

You could try a video log: sit in front of a video camera each day and talk about the previous 24 hours, or record a voice-over as the camera explores the physical memorabilia of the day.

The key here, as with all our suggestions (and, for that matter, life itself), is flexibility and fun.

A second key is: do whatever you'll *consistently do*. Don't start an Epic Production that will be abandoned in a short while (with the best intentions of returning to it, of course). Build up to that. For now, you might start by scribbling a note or two in the margins of this book as you go along.

*I'm going to
turn on the light,
and we'll be two people
in a room
looking at each other
and wondering
why on earth we were
afraid of the dark.*

GALE WILHELM

Light

Whatever that invisible force is that responds to human interaction, that's what we mean by light.

It could be the mysterious something that makes subatomic matter appear as particles to scientists expecting them to be particles, and as waves to scientists expecting them to be waves.

It could be the force at the core of almost all religions and spiritual pursuits. (The term "light" is often used to describe this phenomenon.)

We're not going to "take sides" here—that information is part of The Gap. We have, however, found that—whatever the reason—using the light seems to work. *Why* it works is not the subject of this chapter. *That* it works, and more importantly, how to work it, is.

If you've used the light before, you know it works. This will be a reminder. If you've never used light, then consider this chapter the parameters of an experiment. Please neither believe nor disbelieve the effectiveness of this tool; simply try it in a variety of situations, and see what happens.

Using the light is very easy. You simply ask that the light (you can imagine it as a clear, pure white light) be sent somewhere for the highest good of all concerned. That's it. That's using the light.

In fact, light can't be "sent"—it's all around all the time everywhere anyway. In a sense, it's as silly to "send" light as it is to "send" air. (When we were traveling in Israel, however, we did buy a can of "Air From the Holy Land.") We do ask that the light that's already there (or here) to "do its thing" for the highest good.

How do we know the light "worked"? Sometimes the situation changes, sometimes our attitude about the situation changes, and sometimes both.

Things may not change the way we want them to change. The light is not a bellhop in the sky. It will not do what you want at the expense of others—or yourself. As Oscar Wilde pointed out, "When the gods choose to punish

Man is his own star,
and the soul that can
Render an honest and a
perfect man
Commands all light,
all influence, all fate.

JOHN FLETCHER
1647

us, they merely answer our prayers." To have *all* of our desires fulfilled would be a curse.

That's where the "highest good" part comes in. We don't always know what the highest good is. (Although we often *think* we do or *feel* we do—and haven't our thoughts and feelings been wrong in the past?) That's why we suggest that, when you use the light, you add "...for the highest good of all concerned." The "highest good" is the safety clause. We don't want to play Sorcerer's Apprentice with our lives.

Using the light doesn't require an elaborate ritual or procedure. It takes almost no time. You can get it down to three words: "light, highest good." If you're concerned about someone or something add, "light, highest good," to the concern, and let it go. Then, if you so choose, get involved in improving the situation. If you choose not to get involved physically, send the light and let it go. You've done all that you can do, which, you may find, is quite a lot.

In what situations can you use the light? In what situations can you use air? We can't imagine a situation in which you *couldn't* use the light. Just before dropping off to sleep, some people ask for the light to surround, fill, protect, bless and heal them, for their highest good and the highest good of all concerned. When they wake up, they ask the light not only to be with them, but also to go ahead of them, preparing each experience of the day for their highest good.

Using light is not a religion, any more than using air is a religion. People who claim it as an exclusive part of their doctrine might as well claim that only its believers can enjoy the benefits of air. The light can be used as an adjunct to any religious or spiritual path you are on or may find yourself on in the future; or it can be used in a purely ecumenical, secular way.

Eventually, using the light becomes as automatic as breathing.

See golden days,
fruitful of golden deeds,
With Joy and Love
triumphing.

JOHN MILTON

1667

Visualization

In a sense, it's unfortunate the term *visual*ization has become the almost-exclusive word for any work done in the imagination. The word visual is, of course, connected to sight. People try a moment or two of *"visual*ization," say they never "saw" anything, and give up. When they hear about the wonders of visualization, they assume it's another one of "those things" that other people have, but they don't.

Actually, a great many people never "see" a thing during visualization. Others have murky images. Some only have a "sense" or feeling of things. Others hear the "images." Few people, in fact, see the crisp, clear, Technicolor images we assume most everybody (but us) sees.

We all "visualize." If we were to ask you to draw a circle, you could do it. A circle is a visual thing. You had to "envision" it somehow. However you "saw" the circle in your imagination, that's how you'll "see" while visualizing.

Don't remember how you "saw" the circle? Try a triangle. How about a square? "It's just *there*," you might say. Or maybe you notice, "It takes a little while, but then it appears." All these are fine.

Now graduate school. Think of the Eiffel Tower. The Statue of Liberty. The moon. An orange. A lemon. A lake. A rose. What color is the rose? Is it a red, red rose, or are you from Texas? Some people get an "image" instantly, some take as long as five seconds each. (And five seconds can seem like a long time.) However you got these—be it a sense, feeling, verbal description, or an image—that's how you visualize.

Most of us spend a great deal of time believing *visual lies*. We have an image of our unworthiness, believe it, and that gives birth to one imagined failure after another. The unworthiness is a lie, but the projected failures can come true: what we focus upon we can become.

With visualization, you begin to tell yourself visual truths.

I discovered the
"something"
in
"nothing."

BARBRA STREISAND

The Sanctuary

A sanctuary is an inner retreat you build with visualization in your imagination. Here you can discover the truth about yourself, and work to affirm it. ("Make it firm.")

We call it a sanctuary. Some call it a workshop, or an inner classroom. You can call it whatever word gives you the sense of asylum, harbor, haven, oasis, shelter—a place you can go to learn your lessons in peace and harmony. We refer to it as a sanctuary.

There are absolutely no limits to your sanctuary, although it's a good idea to put some limits on it. In this way, the sanctuary is a transitional point between the limitations of our physical existence and unlimitedness.

The sanctuary can be any size, shape or dimension you choose—large and elaborate or small and cozy. It can be located anywhere—floating in space, on a mountain top, by an ocean, in a valley, anywhere. (You are welcome to combine all those, if you like.) The nice thing about the sanctuary: you can change it or move it anytime—instantly.

The sanctuary can contain anything you choose. We'll suggest some things here, but consider this just the beginning of your shopping list. Before giving our design tips (you can consider us interior designers—with an emphasis on the word interior), we'll talk about ways in which you might want to "build" your sanctuary.

Some people will build theirs by simply reading the suggestions: as they read each, it's there. Others might read them over now for information, and then put on some soft music, close their eyes and let the construction begin. Still others may want to make this an *active* process. With their eyes closed (and being careful not to bump into too much furniture), they might physically move as each area of the sanctuary is built and used. All—or any combination—of these is, of course, fine.

While reading through our suggestions, you will probably get ideas for additions or alterations. By all means make notes of these, or simply incorporate them as you

*Imagination is more important
than knowledge.*

ALBERT EINSTEIN

*The doctor can bury his mistakes
but an architect can only advise
his client to plant vines.*

FRANK LLOYD WRIGHT

1869-1959

go. Have we gotten across the idea that this is *your* sanctuary? OK, let's go.

Entryway. This is a door or some device that responds only to you and lets only you enter. (We'll suggest a way to bring others into your sanctuary in a moment.)

Light. Each time you enter your sanctuary, a pure, white light cascades over you, surrounding, filling, protecting, blessing and healing you—for your highest good, and the highest good of all concerned.

Main Room. Like the living room of a house or the lobby of a hotel, this is the central area. From here, there are many directions to go and many things to explore.

People Mover. This is a device to move people in and out of your sanctuary. No one ever enters without your express permission and invitation. You can use an elevator, conveyor belt, *Star Trek* beam-me-up device, or anything else that moves people. Let there be a white light at the entry of the mover as well, so that as people enter and leave your sanctuary, they are automatically surrounded, filled, protected and healed by that white light, and only that which is for their highest good and the highest good of all concerned is taking place.

Information Retrieval System. This is a method of getting any kind of information—providing, of course, it's for your highest good (and the highest good of all concerned) that you have it. The Information Retrieval System can be a computer screen, a staff of librarians, a telephone, or any other device from which you feel comfortable asking questions and getting answers.

Video Screen. This is a video (or movie, if you like) screen in which you can view various parts of your life—past, present or future. The screen has a white light around it. When you see images you don't like or don't want to encourage, the light is off. When the screen displays images you want to affirm, the light glows. (Those who are old enough to remember Sylvania's Halo of Light television know just what we mean.)

Ability Suits. This is a closet of costumes that, when worn, give you the instant ability to do anything you want to do—great actor, successful writer, perfect lover, eager learner, Master of your Universe; any and all are

*If you have built
castles in the air,
your work need not be lost;
that is where they should be.*

*Now put the foundations
under them.*

HENRY DAVID THOREAU

available to you. When you're done with an Ability Suit, just throw it on the floor in front of the closet—Ability Suits have the ability to hang themselves up.

Ability Suit Practice Area. This is a place you can try new skills—or improve upon old ones—while wearing your Ability Suits. Leave lots of room, because there's an Ability Suit for flying and another for space travel. In your sanctuary, not even the sky's a limit.

Health Center. Here the healing arts of all the ages—past, present, future; traditional and alternative— are gathered in one place. All are devoted to your greater health. The Health Center is staffed with the most competent health practitioners visualization can buy. Who is the most healing being you can imagine? That's who runs your Center.

Playroom. Here, all the toys you ever wanted—as a child or as an adult—are gathered. There's lots of room— and time—to play with each. As with Ability Suits, you never have to worry about "putting your toys away." They put themselves away.

Sacred Room. This is a special sanctuary within your sanctuary. You can go there for meditation, contemplation or special inner work.

Master Teacher. This is your ideal teacher, the being with whom you are the perfect student. The Master Teacher (or MT for short) knows everything about you (has always been with you, in fact). The MT also knows all you need to learn, the perfect timing for your learning it, and the ideal way of teaching it to you. You don't *create* a Master Teacher—that's already been done. You *discover* your Master Teacher. To meet your Master Teacher, simply walk over to your People Mover, ask for your Master Teacher to come forth, and from the pure, white light of your People Mover comes your Master Teacher.

(We'll leave you two alone for a while. More uses for the Sanctuary later. See you both in Part Three!)

*A problem is a chance
for you to do your best.*

DUKE ELLINGTON

PART THREE

MASTER TEACHERS
IN DISGUISE

Your Master Teacher—as wonderful as your MT is—is not the only Master Teacher in your life. Far from it.

Most people think Master Teachers are only "in the skies." Not so. They're here, there and everywhere. Why don't we recognize them as such? Because they are also masters of disguise.

How do they disguise themselves? Only as some of the most potentially powerful learning tools in our lives: mistakes, guilt, resentment, fear, pain, stubbornness, addictions, disease, death, depression, overweight, emergencies—all the things most people would, if they could, eliminate.

Some try awfully hard to eliminate them, too. Ever notice the themes of some best-selling books? How to get rid of this Master Teacher, how to dispose of that Master Teacher, 26 ways to eradicate some other Master Teacher.

Why would we want to remove sources of wisdom from our lives? Maybe we forgot that they were Teachers—or maybe nobody ever explained it to us.

Let's pretend your Master Teachers sent us here to explain what they have to offer you; what great friends they truly are. That way maybe you'll use them and stop trying to get rid of them. Consider us the goodwill ambassadors for Master Teachers in Disguise Guild.

There is a funny scene from the musical *Showboat*. Two mountain men, who have never seen a play, stumble into the showboat theater, unaware that the actors are

Shall I crack any of
those old jokes, master,
At which the audience
never fail to laugh?

ARISTOPHANES

405 B.C.

acting in a play. They converse with the heroine and encourage the hero. When the villain arrives, they chase him off the stage with six-guns. The mountaineers are proud of themselves for having done "the right thing."

The irony in this, of course, is that the audience, watching *Showboat*, forgets the men playing the mountaineers are actors, too. The audience laughs at the naiveté of people mistaking real-life for play-acting. In order to appreciate the humor, however, the audience watching *Showboat* must be lost in the illusion themselves.

That's how the Master Teachers get away with the disguise: we forget—and seldom are we interested in remembering again. If someone stood up during a performance of *Showboat* and began yelling, "Those aren't mountain men! Those are actors! Those aren't real guns! Those are props!" the person would be unceremoniously ushered from the theater.

The Master Teachers need the illusion of reality to teach us their lessons as well as they do. The more we believe the reality of the characters in the movie we're watching, the more moving the movie can be. Thus, the more we believe the Master's disguise, the more powerful and complete the lesson.

So why are we spilling the beans?

If you're struggling too much with the teacher, you might not stand back and learn the lesson. The techniques in this section of the book allow you to take that step back. You can learn from past Master Teaching sessions (all that you might have considered the doom and gloom of your past). You can also use the techniques to more quickly learn the ongoing lessons being taught by your MT's.

But by exposing the Master Teachers (the "villains" of the piece) as the wonderful, kindly, loving friends they are, aren't we risking the effectiveness of future lessons?

Not likely.

You'll forget all this.

*Experience is the name everyone
gives to their mistakes.*

OSCAR WILDE

*Mistakes are
the portals of discovery.*

JAMES JOYCE

Mistakes

One of the least disguised of the Master Teachers in Disguise is mistakes. Mistakes, obviously, show us what needs improving. Without mistakes, how would we know what we had to work on?

This seems an invaluable aide to learning, and yet many people avoid situations in which mistakes might take place. They also deny or defend the mistakes they've made—or may be making.

There is a story told of Edison who made, say, 1,000 unsuccessful attempts before arriving at the lightbulb. "How did it feel to fail 1,000 times?" a reporter asked. "I didn't fail 1,000 times," Edison replied. "The lightbulb was an invention with 1,001 steps."

Why don't most of us see our own lives in this way? We think it goes back to unworthiness. We assume a façade of perfection in a futile attempt to *prove* our worthiness. "An unworthy person couldn't be this perfect," the facade maintains. Alas, being human, we make mistakes. Mistakes crack the façade. As the façade crumbles, a frantic attempt is made to hide the hideous thing (unworthiness) the façade was designed to hide—from ourselves as much as from others.

If we didn't play this game of denial with ourselves, we would make mistakes when we make them, admit them freely, and ask not, "Who's to blame?" or "How can I hide this?" but "What's the lesson here? How can I do this better?"

The goal becomes excellence, not perfection.

One of the best examples of how strong the taboo against making a mistake has become is the use of the word sin. In Roman times, sin was a term used in archery. It meant simply to miss the mark. At target practice, each shot was either a hit or a sin. If you sinned, you made corrections and tried again.

Today, of course, sin means, to quote the American Heritage, "A condition of estrangement from God as a result of breaking God's law." Whew. No wonder people

Aim for success,
not perfection.
Never give up your right to
be wrong, because then you
will lose the ability to learn
new things and move
forward with your life.
Remember that fear always
lurks behind perfectionism.
Confronting your fears and
allowing yourself the right
to be human can,
paradoxically, make you a
far happier and
more productive person.

DR. DAVID M. BURNS

avoid even "the near occasion" of sin. Some people treat mistakes with the same reverence.

Mistakes are valuable if, for no other reason, they show us what *not* to do. As Joseph Ray told us, "The Athenians, alarmed at the internal decay of their Republic, asked Demosthenes what to do. His reply: 'Do not do what you are doing now.'"

In Hollywood, mis-takes are common. ("That was wonderful, darlings. Now let's get ready for take two.") Give yourself as many re-takes as you need. Stars do it. ("I didn't feel quite right with that one, Mr. DeMille. Can we take it again?") Why not you?

A Hollywood song (lyrics by Dorothy Fields) sums it all up, "Pick yourself up, dust yourself off, start all over again." Or, to quote an African proverb, "Do not look where you fell, but where you slipped."

If you're learning, growing and trying new things—expect mistakes. They're a natural part of the learning process. In fact, someone once said, "If you're not making at least 50 mistakes a day, you're not trying hard enough." What the person meant, we think, is that growth, discovery and expansion have mistakes built into them.

To avoid situations in which you might make mistakes may be the biggest mistake of all.

I hate quotations.

RALPH WALDO EMERSON

The Two Faces of Anger:
Guilt and Resentment

Guilt is anger directed at ourselves—at what we did or did not do. Resentment is anger directed at others—at what they did or did not do.

The process of guilt and resentment is the same:

1. We have an image that either we or others should live up to. (An image of all the should's, must's, have-to's and demands we learned or created about our own and/or others' behavior.)

2. We placed an emotionally-backed demand that we or others must live up to this image.

3. We or they fail to live up to our image.

4. We judge the "contrary action" as wrong, bad, evil, wicked, etc.

5. We become emotionally upset—bitter, alienated, hurt, hostile, belligerent, combative, contentious, quarrelsome, vicious, touchy, cranky, cross, grouchy, testy, enraged, aggravated, annoyed, furious, teed-off, etc., etc. We'll put them all under the general umbrella of "angry."

6. We assign blame for the emotional upset—either *we* did it or *they* did it. (The judge pronounces sentence.)

7. The swift execution of justice. If we are to blame, we direct the anger toward ourselves, feeling regret, remorse, shame, repentance, culpability, fault—we'll call all that guilt. If the transgressor of our expectations was someone or something other than ourselves, we call our anger spiteful, jealous, suspicious, malicious, begrudging, covetous, envious, indignant—all of which we'll call resentment. The sad fact is that, whether we blame *us* or *them*, it's *us* who hurts. That is not considered. If it is considered, it is not considered for long.

*Every great mistake has
a halfway moment,
a split second when it
can be recalled and
perhaps remedied.*

PEARL S. BUCK

8. All of this continues for the prescribed length of time and intensity. No reprieves, no appeals—*possible* time off for *very* good behavior.

If these are the two faces of anger, what's the good in that? Frankly, not much. So why do we have it in a section on Master Teachers? If we listened to the voices of the Master Teachers at the very beginning, the feelings of guilt and resentment—those hurtful/hurting feelings that can go on for years—would not have been necessary. To save us from this is the job of the Master Teacher of anger.

Anger, as guilt and resentment, begins as an inner twinge. We sense something long before it blossoms (explodes?) into an emotional tirade. If we listen to this twinge—and follow its advice—the emotional outburst (or inburst) is not needed.

What advice is this MT giving? Stop, look and change.

Stop. Don't do anything. You are at a choice point. You have two ways to go. One choice equals freedom. The other choice equals misery—familiar misery; maybe even comfortably familiar misery, but misery nonetheless.

Look. What image (expectation, belief, should, must, ought-to, etc.) about either yourself or another is about to be (or has recently been) violated? ("People *should* drive carefully," "I *mustn't* eat cake if I'm on a diet," etc.)

Change. What do you change? The image. Your image—based upon hard, cold, physical evidence—*is not accurate*. People *should* drive carefully, but do they always? Hardly. That "should" is inaccurate, false, erroneous, wrong. People on diets *mustn't* eat cake, but do they? You bet. That "mustn't" is untrue, faulty, mistaken and incorrect. Based upon the actual life-data given to you, your images (should's, must's, have-to's, etc.) are all wet (or don't hold any water—or any other aquatic metaphor you choose.)

But what do we often do with the image that is proven—conclusively—to be inaccurate? Do we disregard it? Do we intelligently alter it, based upon reality? ("People should drive carefully, and sometimes they don't." "People on diets shouldn't eat too much cake too

*Everything that irritates us
about others can lead us to
an understanding
of ourselves.*

CARL JUNG

often, except when they do.") No. We make ourselves miserable with the inaccurate image. The world's actions do not conform to our beliefs. Woe is us. Our own actions don't conform to our beliefs. Woe *on* us.

Can you see the absurdity of this? We demand that our illusion (our image) is more real than reality (what actually happened), hurting ourselves in the process. Where is the victory in that? (We bet you thought that was a rhetorical question. It's not. There are answers.)

First, we get to feel right. Feeling right is a strong drug. Some people sacrifice a lot to be right. Ever hear the expression "dead right"? Our question: Would you rather be right or be happy? That's the question the Master Teacher asks with each initial twinge of guilt or resentment. If we answer "Happy," we are free. If we answer "Right," the cycle of misery begins again. If we're right we must punish—either ourselves or another. As we mentioned, the irony is that when we punish another, we first punish ourselves. Who do you think feels all that hate we have for another? The other person? Seldom. Us? Always.

Second, it's a habit. We learned it early on—before we could walk or talk, in some instances. The habit is so ingrained in some people that they haven't understood a word of this chapter. "What *are* they talking about? When people do something *wrong*, I will *naturally* feel upset. When I do some thing *bad*, I will *of course* feel guilty." It's not "natural," it's not "of course"; it's learned. If our early lessons of acceptance were as successful as our early lessons of anger, how much happier we would all be.

Third, it gives us (and others) permission to do it again. Far from preventing a recurrence, the punishment simply lets the person (either yourself or another) say, "I've paid my dues, now I'm free to do it again." Many people weigh the guilt they will feel against the pleasure of the self-forbidden action they want to take. As long as they're willing to "pay the price," the action's OK. People often ponder the anticipated wrath of another before taking certain actions. "If I'm five minutes late, they'll be a little mad." They make a choice between another's resentment and whatever it is that might make them five minutes late. If they're willing to endure the chastisement,

The last temptation is the greatest treason:
To do the right deed for the wrong reason.

T. S. ELIOT

they reason, it's OK to be late. Guilt and resentment, then, far from preventing "evil" ("live" backwards), perpetuates it.

What if we use the twinge of guilt to change the action? What if we feel the guilt and *not* eat the cake? Isn't this using the Master Teacher's message for our good?

Well, it's a good start. If we don't do something because we're afraid of the guilt, we are, in fact, being motivated by fear and guilt. If we do good because we fear what might happen to us if we don't do good, the act of good is tainted with fear. As a transition—especially when breaking a habit—it's a beginning, but we must move beyond that, or we find ourself in the trap of not feeling guilty because we'd feel guilty if we felt guilty.

So what can we use to motivate us to do good? Do good because good is the right thing to do. Not right as "conforming to law and morality (or else)," but right as "in accordance with fact, reason and truth."

Another great motivator is love. Love yourself enough to stay on the diet because you love your body and want to keep it healthy.

More on this and other positive motivators later, along with the cure for guilt and resentment.

The cure for guilt and resentment? Forgiveness. The preventative? Acceptance. The best reason to do good? Loving.

And if you forget any of this, the Master Teacher will be there, just before you veer off-course, asking gently, with that first tinge of guilt or resentment, "Would you rather be right or be happy?"

Your answer will always be respected.

Don't be afraid to take
a big step
if one is indicated.
You can't cross a chasm in
two small jumps.

DAVID LLOYD GEORGE

Fear

When entering a new situation, wouldn't it be wonderful to have a burst of extra energy? Wouldn't it be nice if our senses sharpened, our mind became more alert, and we felt a sense of increased readiness? Wouldn't it be great if we breathed a little deeper, getting more oxygen into our body; our heart beat a little faster, getting that oxygen around our body; and our eyes widened a little, allowing us to see more clearly?

Wouldn't that be a nice gift to have? That would be a Master Teacher worth welcoming, right?

Well, we have that gift already. It's called fear.

Fear? Sure. If you think about it (or perhaps we should say *feel* about it), the only difference between "fear" and "excitement" is what we label it. The two are pretty much the same physiological/emotional reaction. With fear, we put a negative spin on it: "Oh, no!" With excitement, we give it some positive english: "Oh, boy!"

Why does fear have such a bad rap? Childhood. Our parents used fear to keep us safe when we were out of their sight. As children, we didn't know the difference between playing in the street and playing on a playground; we didn't know the difference between poison and milk; we didn't know the difference between a total stranger and a perfect stranger. Our parents taught us—with the most loving intentions—to fear *everything* new.

This fear probably saved our lives on any number of occasions. "When in doubt, don't." We didn't, and because we didn't, we're here to tell about not doing it.

All well and good. The problem is, at the age of, say, 18, when we *did* know the difference between the truly dangerous and the merely intriguing, no one taught us to use fear for the remarkable gift it is. It's as though nobody took the training wheels off our bike.

Today, we probably don't need to fear poison to keep us from drinking it. We don't drink it because, well, there's no future in it. Only occasionally do we need the rush of fear necessary to quickly avoid a new situation

Everyone has talent.
What is rare is the courage
to follow the talent to the
dark place where it leads.

ERICA JONG

(an imperfect stranger on a dark street, for example). Most of the time, however, fear is a wonderful ally in our quest for growth, learning and expansion.

To use fear as the friend it is, we must retrain and reprogram ourselves. (Enough blaming the past. Your life is in your hands now.) We must persistently and convincingly tell ourselves that the fear is here—with its gift of energy and heightened awareness—so we can do our best and learn the most in the new situation.

Before we can make friends with fear, it may be necessary to learn that fear is not the enemy. We must know that, if we do the thing we fear, we will not die. Some people tell themselves, of every new situation, "It's going to be awful and terrible and then I'll die." The phrase "to die of embarrassment" is an example of the exaggerations people believe about fear.

To prove to ourselves we won't die—that, in fact, nothing physically bad is likely to happen to us—it's necessary to walk through the fear. Most people treat fear as a wall. It is the edge of their comfort zone. As they approach the wall and the fear increases, they turn around and walk away. They do not do the thing they fear. Hence, the belief that fear is a limitation, and not a prelude to illumination, is perpetuated.

If you want to learn about fear, whatever it is you fear doing, that is the very next thing you need to do. Fear is not a wall; it's just an emotion. Walk through the fear. Keep taking step after step toward the thing you want. It may become quite uncomfortable; then, suddenly, it will be less.

Once you start doing the thing you fear, the fear is used for its true purpose: extra energy. We use the energy doing the thing we want to do, and the "wall" sensation of fear disappears.

Over time, you'll learn to use the energy even before you start moving—you'll create a gate for yourself in the wall. Then, when the fear arises, you'll say, "Welcome. I needed a little extra energy. This one might be a challenge!" And off into the sunrise you'll go with your old friend.

If I had a formula
for bypassing trouble,
I would not pass it round.
Trouble creates
a capacity to handle it.

I don't embrace trouble;
that's as bad as treating it
as an enemy.

But I do say
meet it as a friend,
for you'll see a lot of it
and had better be
on speaking terms with it.

OLIVER WENDELL HOLMES

Pain and Dis-ease

Imagine this scenario: You have a very important appointment at 9:00 a.m. The night before, you tell your two roommates, who are also two of your best friends, "I have an important meeting tomorrow morning. It means a lot to me. Would you please make sure I'm awake by 8:00 a.m.?" Your friends, knowing your history of sleeping late, are reluctant. "Please do it," you implore, "It's very important. Do whatever you have to, just make sure I'm up by 8:00 a.m." Your friends agree.

The next morning at 7:00, they knock on your door. You do not respond. Five minutes later they knock harder. No response. Five minutes later they knock and yell. No response. Ten minutes later they come into your room and yell. No response. Five minutes later they gently shake you. You tell them to leave you alone. You've changed your mind. The appointment's not so important after all. Knowing you well, they do not believe you. Ten minutes later they shake you and call your name. You inform them you are awake. They are not convinced. They check back in ten minutes: still asleep. As 8:00 a.m. approaches, they shake you, yelling, "Wake up!" You are not pleased. Your friends are threatening cold water. Eventually, reluctantly—if your friends are good enough (i.e., persistent enough)—you wake up.

What if this were the role pain and dis-ease played in your life? We may not remember giving a wake-up call, and we may not remember asking these two to do the awakening, but doing it they are.

What are we waking up to? Ourselves. Living in the moment. Living life more effectively. Better relationships with ourselves and others. And so on. When we're "asleep," we are unconscious and not aware of these things. Our friends know we want to be aware of them, and so they go through the thankless job of waking us up.

Pain (any pain—emotional, physical, mental) has a message. The information it has about our life can be remarkably specific, but it usually falls into one of two categories: "Our life would be more alive if we did more of this," and, "Our loving would be more lovely if we did less

Whenever he
thought about it,
he felt terrible.
And so, at last, he came to
a fateful decision.
He decided
not to think about it.

of that." Once we get the pain's message, and follow its advice, the pain goes away.

You can use your sanctuary to find out what your pain is trying to tell you. You can, for example, contact the pain through the Information Retrieval System. Or you could have it appear on the Video Screen. You might have to "consult" with it in the Health Center. You can invite it in on the People Mover.

Imagine the pain as though it were animated by Walt Disney, or maybe as a Muppet puppet. Give it a mouth. Let it speak. Remember, this is a friend. Ask it a few questions. For example:

What do I get from having you around? What excuses do you give me? What information do you have for me? What should I be doing less often? What should I' be doing more often? How can I better take care of my body? How can I better take care of my emotions? What can I do to better take care of my mind? What can I do to better take care of myself?

After you've had your chat, thank the pain for the information, surround it with white light, and see it dissolve into that light. Then fill the place in your body/mind/emotions where the pain was with white light.

It is important to follow the pain's advice. Remember, painful = PAY-IN-FULL. The more severe the pain or illness, the more severe will be the necessary changes. These may involve breaking bad habits, or acquiring some new good ones. To hear the advice of the pain without following it is as useful (or should we say useless?) as any other unheeded good advice. Take the corrective action necessary, and the pain will decrease. Continue this healing-through-action, and you will be healed.

How far will pain go to get its message across? Illness. Dis-ease. The ultimate wake-up call is a life-threatening illness. If that alarm clock in your ear doesn't wake you up, nothing will. (Our book on this subject, *You Can't Afford the Luxury of a Negative Thought: A Book for People with Any Life-Threatening Illness—Including Life,* is available by calling 1-800-LIFE-101. Naturally, we recommend it highly.)

*It's a funny thing about life;
if you refuse to accept
anything but the best,
you very often get it.*

SOMERSET MAUGHAM

Stubbornness

Gather 'round rebels, this chapter's especially for you. (Considering our temperaments, we should probably say "us.")

Many rebels got into the rebellion business for good reason—they were rebels with a cause. As a child, when the world moved in with its obsession for conformity ("We'd love you a lot more if only you were a little less different"), the rebel said, "I won't," and stuck to it.

The defense of their individuality continued—probably necessarily so—through formal schooling. Eventually it became a habit. They became masters of "won't power." Give them something to be *against* and they shine. As soon as what they're against has gone, they're lost.

Rebels without something to be against are a sad sight. They wander around. They mutter to themselves. They secretly hope something will go wrong so they can be against it. Like professional soldiers in peacetime, rebels would probably be very unhappy in Utopia.

Fortunately, there is a solution. Just as fear is also excitement, stubbornness is also determination. It's simply a matter of shifting the focus from "won't power" to "will power."

Rather than, "I won't get fat," change it to, "I will keep a healthy, slim body." Replace, "I won't be with people who don't understand me," with, "I will be with people who like me the way I am." Turn, "I hate war," to, "I love peace."

It's a matter of finding the positive opposite (and rebels are *so* good at finding opposites) and focusing on that. This shifts the energy from stubbornness to determination.

Our only problem: how do we communicate all this to our fellow rebels in a way that they won't rebel against?

Blessed is the man
that endureth temptation:
for when he is tried,
he shall receive the crown of life.

JAMES 1:12

When you stop drinking,
you have to deal with this
marvelous personality
that started you drinking
in the first place.

JIMMY BRESLIN

Subtracting Addiction

We've all got one—an addiction, that is. There are the well-known addictions: drugs, alcohol, smoking, gambling. There are the less-known-but-getting-more-well-known-each-day addictions: food, sex, romance, work, religion, spirituality—almost anything good can be turned bad by fixation and lack of moderation. Some people are addicted to their negative thoughts and the feelings those thoughts produce.

Some minimize their addiction by calling it a "bad habit." Others deny their addiction to the point of being addicted to denial. Many, who wouldn't dream of having an addiction, are addicted to normalcy. We all have one.

An addiction is anything that has more power over you than you do. If it "runs" you, it's an addiction. If you're not sure it's addiction, stop doing it. If you can stop for an indefinite period of time, then it's a preference, not an addiction. If you can't—or can't even conceive of giving it (them) up—that's addiction.

The "old" word for addiction was temptation. "Lead us not into temptation" (Jesus); "My temptation is quiet" (Yeats); "I can resist everything except temptation" (Oscar Wilde).

Once you're tempted, you've already fallen. The only question is: how far are you going to fall before you get back up?

By far the most successful program for overcoming addiction is the Twelve Steps. Originally created to help alcoholics, the Twelve Steps have been adapted for every known addiction. The program has benefited millions.

THE TWELVE STEPS

1) We admitted we were powerless over our addiction—that our lives had become unmanageable.

2) Came to believe that a Power greater than ourselves could restore us to sanity.

*Why comes temptation, but for
  man to meet
And master and make crouch
  beneath his foot,
And so be pedestaled in triumph?*

ROBERT BROWNING

*A good many young writers
make the mistake of enclosing a
stamped, self-addressed envelope,
big enough for the manuscript
to come back in.
This is too much
of a temptation to the editor.*

RING LARDNER

3) Made a decision to turn our will and our lives over to the care of this Higher Power, *as we understood Him, Her, or It.*

4) Made a searching and fearless moral inventory of ourselves.

5) Admitted to our Higher Power, to ourselves, and to another human being the exact nature of our wrongs.

6) Were entirely ready to have our Higher Power remove all these defects of character.

7) Humbly asked our Higher Power to remove our shortcomings.

8) Made a list of all persons we had harmed, and became willing to make amends to them all.

9) Made direct amends to such people wherever possible, except when to do so would injure them or others.

10) Continued to take personal inventory and when we were wrong, promptly admitted it.

11) Sought, through prayer and meditation, to improve our conscious contact with our Higher Power *as we understood Him, Her, or It,* praying only for knowledge of our Higher Power's will for us and the power to carry that out.

12) Having had a spiritual awakening as the result of these steps, we tried to carry this message to others and to practice these principles in all our affairs.

Once you overcome your addiction, you know you can overcome all things. The impossible becomes possible. The undoable, doable. The unmanageable, manageable. It even eases the process of releasing our addiction to life at the time of our death.

In the process of overcoming addiction, you learn discipline, self-confidence, humility, appreciation, self-love and forgiveness. Important lessons, these. That's why we consider addiction one of the Master Teachers in disguise.

Death is a friend of ours;
and he that is not ready
to entertain him is
not at home.

FRANCIS BACON

Death

Death is an enormous taboo. It's difficult to discuss it without people giggling nervously, becoming entirely too somber, or saying something like, *"Death?* You're going to talk about *death?* Ick. That's bad taste."

When we tell people that in this chapter we will explore the idea that death is a *friend*—a joyful, freeing process—they're liable to think we're mad. Well, we've been thought mad before—by experts; even by ourselves. We figure in 1,000 years, we'll all be dead. What difference does it make what people say about us today? So why not enjoy ourselves while we're alive?

In our culture, death is like ladies' underwear—unmentionable. No one ever *dies.* They pass away, pass over, or simply pass. They are gone, asleep, at peace or at rest. They have either expired, deceased, or departed (dearly).

Many people feel "icky" thinking about death, so they don't. Who, after all, wants to feel icky? They begin to associate the feeling of icky with death. Then they "know" that death is icky. One should, therefore, not think about death, because there's lots of time to feel icky after you're dead, so why bring the ickyness of death into life?

This is about as much logic as many people apportion to the consideration of death. The problem is, if we don't consider death, we are not fully prepared to consider life. Which brings us to our Pop Quiz on death:

Who said this? "We need to be reminded that there is nothing morbid about honestly confronting the fact of life's end, and preparing for it so that we may go gracefully and peacefully. The fact is, we cannot truly face life until we have learned to face the fact that it will be taken away from us."

(A) Mohandas K. Gandhi
(B) Woody Allen
(C) Thomas Mann
(D) Mark Twain
(E) Billy Graham
(F) Charlie Chaplin
(G) Vladimir Nabokov
(H) Emily Dickinson
(I) John Keats

*Thus, thus, it is joy to pass to
the world below.*

VIRGIL
70-19 B.C.

*Death is just
nature's way of telling you,
"Hey, you're not alive anymore."*

BULL
NIGHT COURT

Answer to Pop Quiz (with commentary):

Gandhi said about death: "We do not know whether it is good to live or to die. Therefore, we should not take delight in living nor should we tremble at the thought of death. We should be equiminded towards both. This is the ideal."

Woody Allen wrote, "Death is one of the few things that can be done as easily lying down. The difference between sex and death is that with death you can do it alone and no one is going to make fun of you."

Thomas Mann pointed out, "The only religious way to think of death is as part and parcel of life; to regard it, with the understanding and the emotions, as the inviolable condition of life."

Mark Twain, on his deathbed in 1910, wrote, "Death, the only immortal who treats us all alike, whose pity and whose peace and whose refuge are for all—the soiled and the pure, the rich and the poor, the loved and the unloved."

Charlie Chaplin (you thought we were kidding? Would we kid about death? Sure we would. But would we kid about Chaplin? Never.) said, "Beauty is an omnipresence of death and loveliness, a smiling sadness that we discern in nature and all things, a mystic communion that the poet feels."

Vladimir Nabokov told us, "Life is a great surprise. I do not see why death should not be an even greater one."

Emily Dickinson, a full 23 years before her demise (oh! We're doing it, too) before her *death*, wrote, "Because I could not stop for Death, / He kindly stopped for me—/ The Carriage held but just Ourselves / And Immortality."

John Keats mixed death and courtship when wooing Fanny Brawne. On July 25, 1819, he wrote her, "I have two luxuries to brood over in my walks, your loveliness and the hour of my death. O that I could have possession of them both in the same minute." (What woman could resist?)

The answer, then, to our Pop Quiz is (E) Billy Graham.

Men fear death
as children fear
to go in the dark;
and as that natural fear
in children is increased
with tales, so is the other.

FRANCIS BACON
1625

One of the situations in which
everybody seems to
fear loneliness is death.
In tones drenched with pity,
people say of someone,
"He died alone." I have never
understood this point of view.
Who wants to have to die and be
polite at the same time?

QUENTIN CRISP

Why then, if all these great people had nifty things to say about death, do we as a culture fear it so?

Once again, we return to those thrilling days of childhood. Most people experienced another's death in childhood. Someone they knew as an active, warm, talkative person was suddenly an unmoving, cold, silent corpse. This death stuff did not look like much fun.

"Why are they lying in that box? Why are they going to put them in the ground (or burn them)? If they've gone to God, why are you so sad?" In the grief, commotion and exhaustion that surrounds dying and its aftermath, a child's questions about death are seldom properly answered.

The more people a child asks, the more conflicting the answers may become. Children are little curiosity machines. They know how to ask all the "right" questions— the ones most adults haven't yet figured out for themselves. In the dialogue between children and adults, only sex is shrouded in as much mystery, embarrassment and confusion as death.

If the child was close to the person (or pet) who died, a child may experience loss for the first time. Death, then, is associated with hurt. The child also sees how the adults behave at death: weeping, wailing, suffering. This death thing must be pretty terrible.

If, in childhood, the death of another took place after a long illness, all the unsightliness of the dying process— hospitals, infirmities, unpleasant sights and smells—is associated with death itself. To a child, seeing someone gradually get sicker and in more pain seems to mean that, after death, the sickness and pain will continue to worsen.

None of this includes the hell-is-waiting-for-you, burning-sulphur, fire-and-brimstone religious training some children get. A child, hearing a list of sins, soon realizes, "If this is all I have to do to go to hell, I'm going to hell."

It's little wonder that a child puts the subject of death on hold. Like homework, if they don't have to think about it, they won't. Many people stopped thinking about death in childhood and haven't sincerely considered it since.

Sleep after toil,
port after stormy seas,
Ease after war,
death after life
does greatly please.

EDMUND SPENSER

1590

This means that many people hold a child's view of death as "true" for themselves as adults. Let's see if we can reeducate that part of ourselves—to mature that inner child about death.

Of course, one's belief about what happens after death falls into The Gap. There are, however, only three major beliefs about death in the entire Gap. One or another of these views fits almost every religious, spiritual, philosophical, agnostic and atheistic group in The Gap.

Interestingly, none of these beliefs has much bad stuff to say about death to an average adult follower of that belief. If there is any nastiness after death, it's going to happen to *them* (the nonbelievers), not to *us* (the believers). To a child, certain aspects of some beliefs might appear terrifying, but to an adult, there's nothing to fear. (In fact, in many cases, death is rather appealing.)

Although we stay away from Gap Matters as a rule, we will make this one suggestion while exploring your Gap: Live by what you believe so fully that your life blossoms, or else purge the fear-and guilt-producing beliefs from your life. When people believe one thing and do something else, they are inviting misery. If you give yourself the name, play the game. When you believe something you don't follow with your heart, intellect and body, it hurts. Don't do that to yourself. Live your belief, or let that belief go.

If you're not actively living a belief, it's not really your belief, anyway—you're just kidding yourself. If you're not actively involved in getting what you want, you don't really want it. You probably *really* believe something else, but may be afraid to admit that to yourself.

Let's take a look at each of the three beliefs about death from an adult point of view. If, as a child, you were told you'd know more about death "when you're older," this may be that time.

Life is purely biological. Once the brain stops working, our sense of aliveness is no more, and that's it. As Dr. Albert Ellis, a proponent of this school of thought, pointed out with his characteristic candor and clarity, "When you're dead, you're f—ing dead!"

As a well-spent day
brings happy sleep,
so life well used
brings happy death.

LEONARDO DA VINCI

Immortality consists largely
of boredom.

COCHRANE
STAR TREK

To a child, the idea of "being no more" may be frightening. Children associate nothingness with the dark. The dark can be frightening to a child. Therefore death is frightening.

As adults, we can probably agree with William Hazlitt when he wrote, "Perhaps the best cure for the fear of death is to reflect that life has a beginning as well as an end. There was a time when we were not: this gives us no concern—why then should it trouble us that a time will come when we shall cease to be? I have no wish to be alive a hundred years ago, why should I regret and lay it so much to heart that I shall not be here a hundred years hence?"

If this is a purely biological life, then who would want to live forever anyway? Imagine living forever, and ever, and ever, and ever, and ever, and ever, and ever, and ever, and ever. If you got bored reading all those "ever's," imagine how quickly you would become bored with an eternal life in a finite universe.

Think about it: if you had infinite time but finite space, eventually you would have explored and experienced every "thing" there was to explore and experience. And then you'd get to start over, and over, and over, and over, and over, and etc.

If you've ever gotten bored with anything you once found fascinating, you'll understand this. If you repeatedly experience anything enough times, you'll probably grow tired of it. All repeated experience requires is enough time. Infinity is enough time.

After enough time, you may find yourself agreeing with the person who, in 1990 B.C., wrote, "Death is in my sight today / As when a man desires to see home / When he has spent many years in captivity." It's from a poem called *The Man Who Was Tired of Life*.

Or, as Mark Twain explained, "Whoever has lived long enough to find out what life is, knows how deep a debt of gratitude we owe to Adam, the first great benefactor of our race. He brought death into the world."

We end the exploration of this portion of The Gap with the words of Albert Einstein, "The fear of death is

For God so loved the world,
that he gave his
only begotten Son,
that whosoever believeth in
him should not perish,
but have everlasting life.

For God sent not
his son into the world to
condemn the world;
but that the world through
him might be saved.

JOHN
3:16-17

the most unjustified of all fears, for there is no risk of accident to someone who's dead."

When you die, you go to heaven or hell. This life is a one-shot opportunity. If we're good, we get paradise forever. If we're bad, we go to hell forever. (Some include a pre-heaven condition, purgatory, for those who weren't bad enough for hell, but not yet good enough for heaven.)

This sounds pretty good. Eternal paradise. Now, this wouldn't become tiresome because, as far as we know, heaven is infinite, and, as far as we know, we are not saddled with physical bodies. This wouldn't be boring. This would be eternal bliss.

"Life is eternal," Rossiter Raymond wrote in his *Commendatory Prayer*, "and love is immortal; and death is only a horizon; and a horizon is nothing save the limit of our sight."

In this belief of death, you rest after a careworn life, but you rest not in nothingness, but in paradise. God, James Johnson imagines, uses death as a sort of chauffeur for the Divine Rest Limo Company: "Find Sister Caroline / And she's tired — / She's weary — / Go down, Death, and bring her to me."

Thomas Fuller, in his 1642 *Life of Monica*, tells of the Saint's death: "Drawing near her death, she sent most pious thoughts as harbingers to heaven; and her soul saw a glimpse of happiness through the chinks of her sickness-broken body."

The Bible, in both Old and New Testaments, has many nice things to say about death. Ecclesiastes 7:1 tells us, "The day of death [is] better than the day of birth." In 1 Corinthians 15:54-55, St. Paul wrote, "Death is swallowed up in victory. O death, where is thy sting? O grave, where is thy victory?"

In Revelation 1:18, Jesus said, "I am he that liveth, and was dead; and, behold, I am alive for evermore, Amen; and have the keys of hell and of death." After reading that, it's hard to understand how anyone calling him or herself a Christian could possibly have any concerns about death. The One you believe in says He has the *keys* to hell and death. If someone who loved you said

*Death is a low chemical
trick played on everybody
except sequoia trees.*

J. J. FURNAS

he had the keys to the grocery store, would you worry about starving?

Islam's book of truth, the Koran, begins by calling God merciful, and at 19:66-67 asks, "Man says: 'How is it possible, when I am dead, that I shall then be brought forth alive?' Does he not remember that We have created him once, and that he was nothing then?"

The Koran 29:64 also states, "The present life is naught but a diversion and a sport; surely the Last Abode is Life, did they but know." Did they but know, there would be no fear of death.

Reincarnation. A portion of us keeps coming back again and again, living lifetime after lifetime in body after body, until all necessary lessons are learned. How do we know when all necessary lessons have been learned? When we stop coming back. VARIATION: We already know all there is to know, but we agreed to forget it for a period of time so we could take part in this great play (either opera, soap opera, horse opera or Grand Ole Opry) called life.

If reincarnation is your belief, you, too, have nothing to worry about. Death is the great liberator, a chance to take off your school clothes (or make-up) and meet with old friends at the malt shop (or corner pub) for drinks and good times.

As the Bhagavad Gita, a holy text of Hinduism—the largest group of reincarnationists outside Southern California—says, "For certain is death for the born / And certain is birth for the dead; / Therefore over the inevitable / Thou should not grieve." (Chapter 2, verse 27)

Or fear.

≈

The factual fact about death is that nobody really knows for sure. Many who have been pronounced clinically dead report the trip to "the other side" as a pleasant journey. Almost all who remember, in fact, describe roughly the same thing: looking down on their now-dead

Death is, to us here, the
most terrible word we know.
But when we have tasted its
reality, it will mean to us
birth, deliverance,
a new creation of ourselves.

GEORGE MERRIMAN

body, lifting away from earth, going through a white tunnel, being met by a loving Master form, having their life shown to them from the beginning, learning lessons from their life experiences, being given a choice to "go on" or to return and continue to "study" on earth, and choosing to go back. Many report meeting loved ones who had previously died.

Some remember all these events, others remember some of them, but the consistency of descriptions from a broad range of individuals—even people from *Ohio*—points to the possibility that death (or at least the transition to death) might not be so bad. (An interesting book on the subject is *Heading Toward Omega* by Kenneth Ring.)

If, as Walt Whitman put it, "Nothing can happen more beautiful than death," why don't we all just kill ourselves?

Good question, especially while reading Whitman. That man seemed to have an *affair* with death. ("The sea lisped to me the low and delicious word death," "Come lovely and soothing death," "Sooner or later delicate death," "Praise! Praise! Praise! For the sure-enwinding arms of cool-enfolding death.")

Suicide is always an option, of course. It is, sometimes, what makes life bearable. Knowing we don't absolutely *have* to be here can make being here a little easier. We do not, however, recommend the exercise of it.

If, as we propose, we are here to learn, then all of life—including that which is so painful we want to die—can be used for learning, upliftment and growth. Sometimes it's only after a painful process is over that we can look back and see what we learned from the situation.

In fact, we seldom know our biggest lessons while they're taking place; our experience of that time is usually confusion, pain and/or discomfort. Like travel, the most exotic lands with the most amazing scenery sometimes means sleeping in tents 200 miles from the nearest toilet. It's when we get back home that we remember the magnificent vistas. As William Burroughs explained, "There are certain things human beings are not permitted to know—like what we're doing."

Arthur Dent: *You know, it's at times like this, when I'm stuck in a Volgon air lock with a man from Betelgeuse, about to die of asphyxiation in deep space, that I really wish I'd listened to what my mother told me when I was young.*

Ford Perfect: *Why? What did she tell you?*

Arthur: *I don't know; I didn't listen.*

THE HITCHHIKER'S GUIDE TO THE GALAXY

Suicide is not a good idea for another reason, too. Before we can learn life's more advanced lessons, we must learn the basics—how to talk, walk, operate a body, read, make a living, etc. That takes *at least* twenty years. (Some people haven't mastered it in 50.) That you're reading this book shows us you've "done your time" in the "basic" school, and you're now ready for the truly challenging stuff. Why waste all that preparation?

Sure, "the other side" is wonderful, but you'll be spending the rest of your death there. As Malcolm Forbes had etched on his tombstone, "While alive, he lived."

While alive, live.

Perhaps the most valuable
result of all education
is the ability to make
yourself do the thing
you have to do
when it ought to be done,
whether you like it or not;
it is the first lesson that
ought to be learned;
and however early a man's
training begins,
it is probably the last lesson
that he learns thoroughly.

THOMAS HUXLEY

Depression

When we say depression, we're not using the word in the clinical sense. We're talking about the depression people refer to when they sigh and say, "I'm depressed." It's also known as feeling blue, gloomy, glum, disheartened, melancholy, forlorn and in the pits. It's the "downs" of the usual cycle of ups and downs.

(If your depression is ongoing or severe, by all means seek medical help at once. We'll be discussing nonclinical depressions in this chapter.)

The simple solution for depression: Get up and get moving. *Physically* move. Do. Act. Get going.

Depression is often caused by a sense of not having accomplished enough. We question the usefulness of what we've achieved in the past, and doubt our ability to achieve anything useful in the future. Self-doubt robs us of our energy. We feel depressed.

We look at all we want to do. It seems overwhelming. We tell ourselves, "I can't do all this," and instantly fulfill our own prophecy by not even trying. The energy drops even more, and the depression deepens.

When we eventually feel we *must* do something, there seems to be so much left undone from our previous inertia that we become confused. The confusion leads to indecision. The indecision leads to, "Oh, what's the use," and more inaction.

At some point, the cycle must be broken by action. Do something—*anything*—physical. If the house is a mess, pick up *one thing*—*any* one thing—and *do* something with it—put it away, throw it out, send it to your brother, something, *anything*. Pick up one more thing. Continue. Eventually, you will have a clean house. Before "eventually," however, the depression will begin to lift.

Yes, depression is a Master Teacher. Its message is, "Get moving. The energy is here. Use it." When you start to move, the energy will meet your movement. But first, you must move. (More on all this in Parts Four and Five.)

*The first thing
I remember liking
that liked me back was food.*

RHODA MORGENSTERN

Overweight

Overweight? What on *earth* is the good news in overweight? What is "overweight"? Excess body fat. What is body fat? Stored energy. The good news about being "overweight" is that you have lots of *stored energy* to do all the things you want to do. It's *your* energy—bought and paid for.

Don't worry about *losing* weight (ugh!), think about *using* weight (oh, boy!).

Overweight and depression often go together. The two are twin Master Teachers. Depression says, "I have all these things to do that I haven't done," and overweight says, "Here's the energy to do them, dear. Let's go." If you let them, they will. (Techniques for helping yourself "let them" are found in the next section, "Tools for Successful Doers.")

Make a list of all the things you want to accomplish, and apportion to each thing on the list your extra pounds. (Think of them as "energy units.") "Clean closet, 1 pound. Clean garage, 2 pounds. Find new job, 3 pounds. Call mother, two ounces. Paint living room, 2 pounds. File personal papers, 1 pound. File personal papers so I can actually find something again, 3 pounds." Get the idea?

The trick, of course, is not to eat more while you're doing more. And the second trick is to do more of the things *you* want to do. You may not *want* to do them, but you *do* want the results. The primary goal is the achievement of what you want. You use your weight to get it.

It might also help to reprogram the part of you that associates food with security, loving, comfort and all those things food really has nothing to do with. Tell yourself, "Eating is good. I eat for energy and for health. For loving (comfort, security, etc.), I will love myself (take a hot bath, tell myself I'm safe, etc.)."

(A good tool for doing this is the *Body Balance* tape packet sold by Mandeville Press. It's $30 plus $4 shipping and handling. Box 3935, Los Angeles, CA 90051 or call 213-737-4055.)

Overweight—don't lose it, *use it!*

When you don't have any
money, the problem is food.
When you have money,
it's sex.
When you have both,
it's health.
If everything is simply jake,
then you're frightened
of death.

J. P. DONLEAVY

Emergencies

There are no emergencies, only *emergences*.

Lessons don't always emerge in a methodical, orderly, systematic way. The time frame is seldom leisurely, steady and unhurried.

In addition to lessons, there are *tests*. Without tests, how can your Master Teachers know which lesson to present to you next? Through tests, they discover what you've learned, as well as what you need work on.

We are, of course, tested all the time. Our successful action is a continual passing of tests. Walking, speaking, tying shoes—all those things that were major challenges at two are today's often-passed tests for most of us. By standing, for example, we pass gravity's ongoing tests. (Yes, gravity is a Master Teacher. So is levity.)

When we are tested in new areas of study, we tend to make more mistakes. That's because we haven't mastered the new area yet. That's OK. We're not *supposed* to have mastered it. We're the *student*, not the master. When the tests happen one at a time, we can often manage them. But when the tests emerge two, three, four, fifteen at a time: emergency!

An emergency is several Master Teachers standing at once and saying, "Pop Quiz!"

When you feel yourself overwhelmed by "problems," take a look at the Master Teachers around you. See the smiling faces of Mistakes, Guilt, Resentment, Fear, Pain, Disease, Stubbornness, Addiction, Death, Depression, Overweight. They're waiting to see how well you do.

Do well. Consider it not a problem, but a challenge. Rise to the occasion. Emerge-and-see.

Ask yourself, "What have I learned about this situation that I can now use?" The answer to that question, and your successful application of it, will lead to the spontaneous emergence of achievement, fulfillment, happiness—and a gathering of justifiably proud Master Teachers.

Decide what you want,
decide what you are
willing to exchange for it.
Establish your priorities
and go to work.

H. L. HUNT

PART FOUR

TOOLS FOR
SUCCESSFUL DOERS

We can learn by doing *anything*. Even if we fail—repeatedly—there's something to be learned from that. Of course, one of the lessons we can learn from failure is, "I want to learn some new ways of doing things so I don't have to fail as much anymore."

Or, perhaps you already are a successful doer and, like all successful doers, you know there's always more to learn about successful doing.

This section focuses more on "outer" achievements. The next section, "To Have Joy and to Have It More Abundantly," highlights methods for "inner" success.

You will notice, however, that most tools can be used for either inner or outer enhancement. The same commitment that allows you to make a million dollars can be used for achieving happiness. The same discipline that allows you to focus primarily on your self-worth can also be used to master scuba diving.

The inner mirrors the outer. The outer mirrors the inner. The techniques that apply to one can usually be adapted successfully to the other.

*My function in life
was to render clear
what was already
blindingly conspicuous.*

QUENTIN CRISP

What Is Your Purpose?

Before taking successful action, you must first know what you want. (If you don't know what you want, how will you know if you've gotten it?) Before knowing what you want, it's good to know why you want it. A good way of knowing why you want something is by knowing your purpose in life.

What is your purpose?

A purpose is something you discover. It's already there. It's always been there. You've lived your life by it, perhaps without fully realizing it. (Although when you do discover it, you will know that you've known it all along.)

It's your bellwether, your personal inner divining rod of truth. It tells you, in any given moment, whether you're living your life "on purpose" or not.

A purpose is a simple, positive statement of why you are here. It usually begins, "I am..." and is only a few words long.

It is not a goal. A goal is something that can be reached. A purpose is a direction, like east. No matter how far east you go, there's still lots more east to travel. Purposes can be used for selecting goals, just as someone traveling east can select certain cities as guideposts along the eastward journey.

A purpose is never achieved; it is fulfilled in each moment that you are "on purpose." You use your purpose to set your course in life. When you are "on course," you are "on purpose."

A purpose is not an affirmation. Affirmations can be created and used to make that creation real. A purpose is not created; it is discovered. You already have a purpose. You have always had a purpose. It has always been the same purpose. Your purpose will—for the remainder of this lifetime, at least—remain the same.

A purpose is like a heart. You don't create a heart, but, like the Tin Man in *The Wizard of Oz*, you can discover the one you've always had.

*The purpose of life
is a life of purpose.*

ROBERT BYRNE

Purposes sound something like this. (Don't use this list to *select* a purpose for yourself. Give yourself the time and the freedom to discover your own. These are just here to give you an idea of what purposes sound like.) "I am a cheerful giver," "I am a happy student," "I am a devoted friend," "I serve the planet," "I am a joyful explorer," "I am a lover of life."

There are many ways to discover your purpose. Here are a few. If one doesn't work, try another. Be patient. The discovery of a purpose can take some time. When you come to know yours, you'll also know it was worth the wait.

1. Make a list of all your positive qualities. This is no time for modesty. (False humility, by the way, is just a form of egoism.) Narrow down each of your good qualities to one or two words. "Loving, giving, joyful, playful, caring, effective, etc." If your list is short, ask friends for their suggestions. Using these words as a starting point, find the two or three that suit you best, and arrange them in sentences starting with "I..." or "I am..." When you discover your purpose, it will "click."

2. Before going to sleep, give yourself the instruction, "When I wake up in the morning, I will know my purpose." Have pen and paper by your bed and, first thing when you wake up, write whatever words are there. It may be your purpose.

3. Go to your sanctuary and ask your Master Teacher.

Once you discover your purpose, we suggest not telling anyone. This keeps it powerful. It also keeps others from saying, "So you're a joyful giver, huh? OK, I'll take five dollars," or "Happy helper? You don't seem very happy to *me*." Life's hard enough without having our purpose on display for the random potshots of the world.

When you know your purpose, it's easier to choose and achieve goals. The litmus test, in fact, of any action is simply, "Does this fulfill my purpose?" If yes, you can choose whether you want to do it or not. If no, you have the same choice. There is, however—as you may already know—a certain value to being "on purpose."

Often people attempt to
live their lives backwards;
they try to have more
things, or more money,
in order to do more of what
they want, so they will be
happier.

The way it actually works
is the reverse.
You must first
be who you really are,
then do what you need to do,
in order to have
what you want.

MARGARET YOUNG

Intention and Desire vs. Method and Behavior

There are some things we want because we really want them. There are other things we want because we think they will give us what we really want. The first category we call intentions or desires. The second category we call methods or behaviors.

For example, you may say, "I want a red sports car." We may say, "Fine, and what do you want from the red sports car?" "I want adventure." The true desire or intention was adventure. The red sports car was the method or behavior to get it.

Another example: If you say, "I want more fun," we might ask, "What can you do to have more fun?" You could then give us a long list of the things you find fun to do. In this case, fun is the intention or desire, your list of fun activities are your methods or behaviors.

We say intention *or* desire because some people prefer one word over another. Intention tends to be a bit more mental, desire a bit more emotional. Use whichever you think is best or feels most comfortable.

You can also use either methods *or* behaviors as the activities and things in which you involve yourself to achieve a desire or intention. A behavior is something you do. A method implies, in addition, a plan or a thing. We know people who can incorporate their red sports cars as extensions of their "behavior," and others who certainly include their behavior in the "method" they use to get what they want. Again, use whatever you think best or feels most comfortable.

The intentions or methods people want are *experiences*. They are contained in words such as freedom, security, power, happiness, self-worth, success, satisfaction, respect, peace of mind, adventure, love.

The methods or behaviors people use to get these are simply *symbols* for "the real thing." They include money, job or career, clothes, cars, house, marriage, family, sex,

One must not lose desires.
They are mighty stimulants
to creativeness, to love,
and to long life.

ALEXANDER BOGOMOLETZ

lovers, physical appearance, educational degrees and travel.

When people want a physical thing—and, yes, a husband, wife, child or lover is a physical thing—they are talking about methods or behaviors. When they discuss inner experiences, they are referring to intentions or methods.

There is absolutely nothing wrong with wanting the symbols. This section, in fact, will suggest many techniques (methods? behaviors?) for getting your fair share of symbols.

It helps, however, to know that the house, car, better body, career, or money you want—yes, even a romantic relationship, religion or spiritual path—is simply a method or behavior to get something else, something inner, something experiential (security, fun, energy, satisfaction, love, knowledge of God, inner peace).

Why does it help to know this? First, if you know the experience you're looking for, you can make whole *lists* of methods and behaviors that might provide it. Love can be found in more places than romantic relationships. Fun can be found without having a million dollars. We can make a lengthy itinerary and "scientifically" investigate it to see if a given method or behavior fulfills a desire or intention. If yes, fine. If no, you've still got a long list to explore. Knowing the experiences you want can dramatically improve the chance of finding the methods and behaviors to fulfill them.

Second, knowing the experiences you seek helps you avoid fear and disappointment. If you *know* you want adventure, and think a red sports car is the way to get it, you also know the sports car is part of a bigger adventure: finding the methods and behaviors that will bring you adventure. If the car does it, fine; add "red sports car" to the list of things that (for now) work. If the car doesn't do it, OK. Next method or behavior, please.

If you think the car is the thing you want, but don't know your true intention or desire behind it, it can be a no-win situation. If it does provide you with adventure, then you can become attached to the car—thinking it's *the car* that's doing it. You can become afraid for its safety.

The last time I saw him
he was walking down
Lover's Lane
holding his own hand.

FRED ALLEN

You are, of course, not afraid for the car but afraid that something might steal adventure from your life. If, on the other hand, the car *didn't* fulfill the unknown something you sought, you could well be disappointed. "All that money..." Either way, no win.

Third, and perhaps most important, you learn that *you* can fulfill your own desires and intentions without much outside help at all. And you can give it to yourself *right now*. Want love? Love yourself. Want joy? Be joyful. Want adventure? The last frontier is the interior.

As you can imagine, if *you* provide *yourself* with the experiences you seek, this significantly decreases the frantic quality many people have when pursuing the symbols of life. "I can't be happy until I get..." "I won't rest until..." "My life isn't complete until I..." There's not a desire or intention we can't fulfill for ourselves, right now.

Ironically, once we have given fully to ourselves, those symbols just seem to *cascade* in. Relationships, for example. Who would you rather be around—a joyful, loving, happy person, or a miserable, needy, unhappy person? Well, so would everyone else. People know this, which is why they *pretend* to be loving, happy, joyful, etc. in order to "catch" someone. (People are not fish. They cannot be "caught." They can be held captive temporarily, that's all.)

When you are genuinely "up" because *you* are the source of your own "upness," people either do or do not relate to you, and whether they do or not is fine. As Frank Sinatra explains "his way" of self-fulfillment, "I bring my own crank." (Many, many techniques for doing this are still to come. The book's not over yet—nor, for that matter, is life.)

You can use your behaviors and methods to discover your intentions and desires. Of each external "thing" you want, ask yourself, "What experience am I looking for?"

Experiences, too, can be like layers of an onion. Pleasure may be on the surface, but that's really a symbol for contentment, which is a symbol for peace of mind. Keep asking, and eventually you'll find experiences that are complete in and of themselves—experiences you're not using to achieve other experiences.

*The greatest pleasure in life
is doing what people say
you cannot do.*

WALTER BAGEHOT

When you discover your fundamental desires and intentions, you'll know what you *really* want. Then, finding methods and behaviors to enhance the experiences you seek is not only easier, it's more fun.

I just want to do God's will.
And He's allowed me
to go to the mountain.
And I've looked over, and
I've seen the promised land.
So I'm happy tonight.
I'm not worried
about anything.
I'm not fearing any man.

MARTIN LUTHER KING, JR.
APRIL 3, 1968

You Can Have Anything You Want, but You Can't Have Everything You Want

When we ask people that simple yet profound question, "What do you want?" they sometimes answer, "I want it all!" We often wonder, "If they had it all, where would they put it?"

There's an awful lot of "all" out there. And there's even more "all" to be experienced inside. The people who say they want "it all" either, perhaps, have not taken the time to explore what they really want, or else don't realize one simple fact of life: "You can have *anything* you want, but you can't have *everything* you want."

Living in a physical body on this planet has some genuine, down-to-earth limitations. First, we can put our body in only one place at one time. Second, there are only 24 hours per day, 365 (or 366) days per year. Third, the human lifetime contains only so many years (150 seems to be tops).

When you think about it, these are significant limitations. The limitations become even more severe when we consider the time spent doing "maintenance" on the body: sleeping, washing, eating—and some of us even have to make money to pay for all that.

We can't have "it all" because "all" is more than our "container" of time and space will hold.

Before you cry, "Foul!" and "Unfair!" too loudly, consider this: You *can* have *anything* you want. Pick the thing you want most and, if it's available, if it doesn't already belong to someone else (who wants to keep it), you can have it.

The history books are full of people who said, "I don't care if everybody thinks it's impossible, *I* think it's possible, I want it, and I'm going to get it (or do it)." And they did.

And you can, too.

*The Wright brothers
flew right through
the smoke screen
of impossibility.*

CHARLES F. KETTERING

The catch? The more unobtainable the "want" you want, the more you will have to sacrifice in order to get it. It's not that you *can't* have it, it's that you'll have to give up many—and maybe all—other things.

We were once on a radio talk show and a woman called in. She said she wanted to be an actress more than anything else, and was quite upset that she hadn't succeeded yet. Our conversation went something like this:

"How much time do you spend on your career?"

"I spend *all my time.*"

"You don't sleep?"

"Of course I sleep."

"Are you in a relationship?"

"Yes, but I only see him four or five nights a week."

"Do you have a job?"

"Well, sure. I have to work to support my two daughters."

"How old are your daughters?"

"Four and eight."

As you can probably guess, this woman actually spent only about an hour a week on her career. This is better than no time at all, but, for the most part, careers in show business require more time than one hour a week. What she meant to say was that she spent all of her *free time* pursuing acting. Unfortunately, it's not likely that an hour a week would give her the success she craved, in the time frame she craved it.

Our advice to her? After establishing that she loved her daughters and loved her boyfriend and had no intention of giving them up, we suggested she be grateful for the choices she had already made, and of her successful implementation of them. We told her there were any number of successful actresses we knew who wish they had two healthy children and a loving romantic relationship. The acting? Make it a hobby.

*Who begins too much
accomplishes little.*

GERMAN PROVERB

Remember, the phrase "spending time" is a precise and accurate one. You only have so much time to spend. Please spend it well. We all have only so much time this time around.

It's as though you were in a large store (earth). You are given enough money (time) to buy *anything* in the store, but not *everything* in the store. You can fit a lot of things in your cart (projects you start). When it comes time to pay, however, if your money runs out, that's it. And this store seldom gives refunds. At best, they may reluctantly buy something back as used merchandise—at a fraction of what you just paid for it.

Some people put a "want" in their cart—a new career, a relationship, a car, a house—and fail to consider its cost: the time it will take to obtain *and maintain* the want. At some point, they may find themselves "out of time."

They like to quote Edna St. Vincent Millay: "My candle burns at both ends; / It will not last the night; / But, ah, my foes, and, oh, my friends — / It gives a lovely light." While reciting it, however, they are secretly worried about the wax dripping on the new rug—which hasn't been paid for yet. They may eventually find themselves quoting Samuel Hoffenstein: "I burned my candle at both ends, and now have neither foes nor friends."

Some protest, "Time is money, and with money you can *buy* time." Up to a limit, that's true. But you can't hire someone to learn for you the skills necessary to perform all of the things you yourself want to do (flying a plane, ballet, race car driving, reading, watching videos, etc.). And do you plan to hire people to spend time with your friends, or to entertain your lover(s)?

At a certain point in most everyone's life—rich, poor, organized, scattered—the wants outnumber the available hours in the day. At that point, a want must go a-wanting.

The solution is preventative: choose carefully at the outset. And be grateful that, although you can't have *everything*, there are some very nice *anythings* awaiting your selection.

*I'd rather have
roses on my table than
diamonds on my neck.*

EMMA GOLDMAN

What Do You Want?

We know you know the "right" answer to this question: "I don't want a red sports car, I want adventure!" Yes, that's good—but, *really*, do you still want the sports car? That's what this chapter is about—the red sports cars of life.

In order to get what you want, it's very helpful to know what you want. If you don't know where you want to go, you probably won't get there.

The key in all this is not *what* do you want, but what do *you* want. When asking people to list the material things they want, they often get lost in glamour: what thing can I have or do that will make me *look good*?

Glamour is a world problem. It's been a problem for millions of years: "My mastodon is better than your mastodon," "My pterodactyl can fly faster than your pterodactyl." Glamour is spending time and energy impressing others with externals.

Be true to yourself when choosing what you want. What would please *you*? If a career is more important than a relationship right now, say so. Just because almost every movie, popular song and toothpaste commercial implies you'll never be a whole human until you have another to share your life with, doesn't mean you have to rearrange *your* priorities. If you'd rather be *making* the movies than making whoopee, that's fine.

Conversely, if what you *really* want is a relationship and a family, but your career-oriented friends find that hopelessly corny—tell 'em you're moving to Iowa where the corn grows tall.

We don't mean to imply that you can't have both a career and a relationship. Some can, some can't. (And some in the latter category haven't realized it yet.) It depends on the price of the relationship, the cost of the career, and your payments on the other items already in your cart. We use relationships and career simply as examples of the kinds of sacrifices people make to the graven image of glamour.

*I'd like a bird for
an old lady of ninety-four.
She had one, but it died
and she doesn't realize it.
She keeps it in a cage,
talks to it, and takes it out
and kisses its head.*

CONTESTANT
QUEEN FOR A DAY

So, what do you want? Would you like a list, from one to ten? Getting that list will take pen, paper, and about an hour. Please follow each step, and please write your answers down. Even if you're *sure* you know what number one is, do you know number five? And number one *may* surprise you.

Actually *doing* this exercise—although easy to do—is something people frequently avoid. People intuitively know that when they choose what they want, (A) they will have to give up some "good ideas" that there is simply not time for, and that makes them sad; and (B) there's a much greater chance that they *will* get the things they truly want, which can be scary. For some, rather than face the loss and the fear, they'll just accept the status quo and continue reading self-help books, thank you very much.

We do encourage you to set your reservations aside and do it anyway. You can always burn the list later.

1. Write down everything you want. Don't worry about order, obtainability or relative importance. As an item comes to mind, write it down. Remember, this is a list of *things*—symbols, methods, behaviors—you want. Experiences go on another list. If you want happiness, what are the things you think would contribute to your happiness? This is a list of those things you want to have, do and be (as in, "Be a doctor").

2. As you make your list, include all the things you currently have that you want to maintain. If you don't want to get rid of something, it will take a certain amount of time to maintain. Your list, for example, may contain, "Maintain car, maintain house, maintain relationship, etc."

3. When you feel the list is complete, set it aside and do something else—anything else. Take a walk, take a nap, eat a peach.

4. Return to the list. Did you think of any more wants during the break? Add them to the list.

*The only thing I ever dream
is that I just won every
beauty contest in the world
and all the people I don't
like are forced to build me
a castle in France.*

STEPHANIE VANDERKELLEN

5. Read the list. Cross off any that seem silly or too trivial. If you know "Walk the dog" is not going to make your top ten, then cross it off. *"Take care of the dog,"* however, might, so leave that one on.

6. With your purpose in mind, read the list again. Cross off any wants that oppose your purpose. If your purpose is "I am a friend to all," then cross off "Send Norman a stink bomb." If you haven't discovered your purpose yet, don't worry. Skip to number seven.

7. Classify each want into one of three categories: (A) those that are *very, very* important to you; (B) those that are *very* important to you; and (C) those that are *merely* important to you. If a want isn't important enough to make at least (C), cross it off.

8. On a clean sheet of paper, copy all your (A's). If there are ten or more, stop. If there are not yet ten, copy all your (B's). If there are ten or more (A's) plus (B's), stop. If there are not ten or more (A's) and (B's), either start over, because your list probably doesn't include all the things you want; or reclassify, because you assigned too few (A's) and (B's).

9. With your new list (the A-B list), choose the *one thing* from that list you want most. Write that on a third sheet of paper. Cross that item off the A-B list. From the remaining items, pick the one that's most important. Write that on the third sheet of paper. Cross it off the A-B list. Do this eight more times. Stop.

10. You should now have ten items written on the third sheet of paper. Look at this list. Are there any that are in *direct opposition* to any other? ("I want to stay married." "I want a divorce.") If there are, cross off the one that's the *lower* on the list of the two. Pick another from the A-B list. That done, recopy the entire list on a clean sheet of paper. Number these one through ten. There's your list. This is what you want.

*Since the mind is
a specific biocomputer,
it needs specific instructions
and directions.
The reason most people
never reach their goals is
that they don't define them,
learn about them, or
ever seriously consider them
as believable or achievable.
Winners can tell you
where they are going,
what they plan to do
along the way,
and who will be sharing the
adventure with them.*

DENIS WAITLEY

What about all those (B's) and (C's)? That's not the thing to focus on right now. Look at your top-ten list. Imagine enjoying each. How will you feel? What will you think? What experiences will you have when these are yours, completely and fully?

It's OK to experience that now.

*A man is not idle because
he is absorbed in thought.
There is a visible labor and
there is an invisible labor.*

VICTOR HUGO

1862

Which Is More Powerful—
the Invisible or the Visible?

Now that you have a list of the top ten material things you would most like, we are now, of course, going to tell you to go get them; get busy; make them happen. *Do it!* Later. First, let's talk about invisible intangibles.

Pop Quiz! True or False: What we can see (the visible) is more powerful than what we can't see (the invisible).

By now, you're good enough "students" to know how to psych out the "teachers." You know that we'll probably pick something other than the obvious, logical answer. And you're right. Even if you couldn't think of an invisible thing that was more powerful than a big, strong visible thing, you still *knew* we were going to say, "Invisible is more powerful." Even if you didn't know why, you'd probably answer the Pop Quiz question False.

Is that cheating? No. That's life. That's using everything for your learning, upliftment and growth. Congratulations! Extra marks if you answered the question right for the "wrong" reason.

What if, however, we had given you an essay exam? What if you had to explain yourself? Quentin Crisp will now tell us how to take care of that:

> If you're taking an essay exam on geography, and the exam could be on any of the countries in the world, study only *one* country, and know it well. Let's say you choose China. When it comes time for the exam, and the question is, "Write 1,000 words on Nigeria," you begin your essay, "Nigeria is nothing like China..." and proceed to write everything you know about China.

So if you had studied, say, "Mistakes," and we asked for 1,000 words on The Visible vs. The Invisible, you could begin your essay, "When talking about the visible and the

We look at it
and do not see it;
Its name is The Invisible.
We listen to it
and do not hear it;
Its name is The Inaudible.
We touch it
and do not find it;
Its name is The Formless.

LAO-TZU

604-531 B.C.

invisible, it's very easy to make a mistake. A mistake, after all, is..." and write 980 additional words on mistakes.

Or, as Mark Twain once said, "Put all your eggs in one basket and WATCH THAT BASKET!"

Completely invisible thus far in this chapter is any sense of direction. "What is the point?" you may wonder, and rightly so. We thought it might be good to have a little transitional patter between the *very* material desires of your top-ten list to the undeniably immaterial ideas of the next chapter.

You see, in the next chapter we plan to take you to the source, the very foundation, ground-zero, the starting point of getting those ten things on your list (and lots of others). We found this transition jarring, so, as a segue, we thought we'd discuss the visible and invisible for a while.

If we observe the world around us, it's easy to see that what we can't see is more powerful than what we can.

Take a look at air, for example. Air is hard to look at, of course, because it's invisible. (In the places where you can see the air, what you're seeing is pollution, not air.)

On earth, air is more powerful than almost anything we know. It contains ample amounts of oxygen for animals, and lots of carbon dioxide for plants. Without it, both would die. It is a life line that is so omnipresent (it's always as close as your next breath), we usually take it for granted. It's essential to our functioning for even the next ten minutes. And yet it's invisible.

"All right," some may say, "What about something physical like a house. You can see a house, and if someone dropped a house on you, it would kill you faster than taking air away from you, so wouldn't a house be more powerful?"

What would make the house fall? Gravity—another of those powerful invisible "forces" we take for granted. If gravity didn't pull the house down, the house would have no power to destroy.

The power of the visible
is the invisible.

MARIANNE MOORE

1941

And what about light? You can't "see" light. It's when light reflects off something that we can see its effects. We can see the glow of the lightbulb, and we can see the light it casts, but we can't see the light traveling from the bulb to the objects it's illuminating.

If the sun radiates enough light to illuminate the earth, why is the space between here and the sun dark? Because the light waves are invisible until they strike something—namely the earth's atmosphere (which is made of our good old invisible friend, air—and held in place by our invisible friend, gravity).

And heat? We can't see heat, but we can certainly feel it. If it wasn't for the invisible atmosphere (air) of our planet, held in place by invisible gravity, holding invisible heat, do you know how cold the earth would be? Cold. About 280 degrees below zero at night.

Coolness is just as important for human survival—and until things approach the freezing point, coolness can't be easily perceived, either.

Can you tell the temperature of a tub of water by just looking at it? Unless it's hot enough to steam or cold enough to freeze, you probably can't. Can you tell how warm or cool a room is by looking at it through a pane of glass? Again, unless there are some clues, probably not.

Looking inside ourselves for a moment, we find that our most powerful inner motivators can't be seen. Love, hate, passion, greed, fear, desire, lust, compassion, charity, goodness—all the emotions that set us into motion can't be seen. The *effects* can certainly be seen, but the emotions themselves, no.

And thoughts, well, thoughts are so invisible (yes, you can "see" your own thoughts, but nobody else can) and so powerful, we think they deserve a chapter all to themselves.

In the province of the mind,
what one believes to be true
either is true
or becomes true.

JOHN LILLY

The Power of Thoughts

Every human achievement—from the Hoover Dam to the book you hold in your hand—began as a single thought. ("Let's build a dam." "Let's write a book.")

That single thought was, of course, followed by millions more. Some were optimistic ("Just what the world needs: another dam!" "Just what the world needs: another book!"). Some were perhaps pessimistic ("Just what the world needs: another dam," "Just what the world needs: another damn book").

On the other hand, thoughts have little power at all. Without touching it, fold over the corner of this page. Think *really hard* about folding over the corner of this page. Without touching it—or allowing anyone else to touch it—fold over the corner of this page. Focus all your mental strength, energy, attention and power on folding over a corner. Either corner is fine. Just fold it over without, in any way, physically touching it.

At this point, many are inventing interesting ways to fold the corner over that fit within the limitations we gave. "Maybe if I rub the book against the floor..." This demonstrates the inventiveness of the human mind—and the knowledge that unless *something* is done physically to the page, the corner is *never* going to be folded over.

If you haven't yet "given up," that's fine. You can spend as much time as you like focusing thought-power alone on folding over the corner of this page. You can call friends. Form groups (whole movements, if you choose) dedicated to sending thoughts to folding the corner over.

Once you realize the point—that thoughts alone aren't going to do it—simply reach up and fold over the corner of this page. You don't have to even "think about it." Just—casually—reach up and fold the corner. It can be a little fold or a big fold—makes no difference.

Please do it, however. There are other points to be made on the next page, and a folded-over corner of this page will help us make them. Corner folded? Great. Please turn the page.

*I have found power in the
mysteries of thought.*

EURIPIDES
438 B.C.

Note the power of thoughts without action. In the physical world, seemingly little.

Note the power of the physical action alone. So powerful as to be almost effortless. Most people didn't have to even work to fold over the corner of a page. It was easy. Without the power of thought to guide it, however, human physical energy is like a mindless gorilla set loose in a nuclear power plant. One can only hope (or pray, as you prefer) the resultant damage is contained within the plant, and that certain buttons in the control room are not randomly pushed.

When thought *and* action are combined, the results are powerful—among the most powerful things on earth. The combination of successful communication—the sharing of thoughts—and physical action can, literally, move mountains.

If our goal were to fold over the corner of the previous page in this book, but we failed to communicate that thought to you, it's doubtful that the corner would have gotten folded over. (If you didn't fold it over, you probably *imagined* folding it over, so please continue to imagine it folded.)

Consider the difficulty *we*—John-Roger and Peter McWilliams—would have had folding over the page in this book at precisely the moment you folded it if we had to do it ourselves. Without your assistance, it would have been a near-insurmountable task.

We would have had to travel from wherever we were to wherever you were, gotten your attention, waited while you read to that page in the book, said, "Excuse us," picked up the book, folded over the corner, handed it back to you, said, "Thank you," and then returned to whatever else we were doing.

With your help, however, it was easy. All we had to do was write a few paragraphs. All you had to do was reach up and fold over the corner. The power of a *successfully communicated thought,* from one human mind to another, is one of the most powerful forces we know.

Does it always work? Nah. You can successfully communicate a thought, and the other person can do nothing about it. You can successfully communicate a thought,

*Thus only can you gain the
secret isolated joy of the
thinker, who knows that,
a hundred years after he is
dead and forgotten,
men who never heard of
him will be moving to the
measure of his thought—
the subtle rapture of a
postponed power, which the
world knows not because it
has no external trappings,
but which to his prophetic
vision is more real than
that which commands
an army.*

OLIVER WENDELL HOLMES, JR.
1886

and the other person may do just the opposite. You can successfully communicate a thought, and the other person may do something about it long after you needed it done.

But when it does work, ah, there is power, grace and magic.

Baseball is fun
for you & me.

There is batting and
fielding and making an out,

There is doubles & triples
and even home runs,

But what I like about
baseball is for the fun.

MATT BOHN
At Age 11

Fielding Your Dreams

How powerful are thoughts that become dreams? Here is an example.

A writer, W. P. Kinsella, sat in Calgary, Canada and had a thought: what if an Iowa corn farmer had a dream, and, combining that dream with action, he was able to reunite a father and a son, one of whom was dead, for a game of baseball?

Kinsella did something about his thought—his dream. He wrote a novel called *Shoeless Joe*. The book was read by film director Phil Alden Robinson. Without ever meeting, the dream (thought) was passed (successfully communicated). Robinson's dream was to write and direct a film based on the book. His dream, too, was for Kevin Costner to play the farmer.

He successfully communicated his dream to Costner, who helped pass the dream along to some money-people in Hollywood. Many successfully communicated dreams later, a film was made—*Field of Dreams*.

It was (and is) a great film, a great success (Hollywood translation: it made a lot of money), and was an Academy Award nominee.

Well and good. But the power of that dream, that thought, doesn't end here.

The farm on which the film was shot is owned by Don Lansing. Since the film's opening, thousands of people, moved by the power of a dream, have traveled to Dyersville, Iowa to see the field, play a little baseball, get married (really, at home plate)—but mostly to affirm that dreams can, and do, come true.

But the story is *still* not over.

(If you haven't seen the film, now is a wonderful time to set down the book, go rent the video, watch it, and return to this spot for the conclusion of this story.)

Here is a letter Lansing received in the fall of 1989....

It's not just my parents
who believe they'll see
Matt on the field, it's me too.
I'll see Matt through my heart.
You have to believe before you
can see things on the field,
and if you believe, you'll see.

STEPHANIE BOHN
AGE 9

I was able to read your letter.
If the movie means anything to
me now it's that you get that
chance to walk with your son.
I am with you in spirit.
Love, Kevin.

KEVIN COSTNER

Dear Don,

You don't know me; my name is Jim Bohn. My son Matt and mother-in-law Lena Blaha died in the crash of United Airlines Flight 232 in Sioux City on July 19.

This past spring I had taken my son and family to see the movie "Field of Dreams." We loved the movie. I had no idea that the "field" was still there. I figured that after the filming it had been replanted. To my surprise and delight, I read an article last evening in our Pittsburgh (Pa.) Press newspaper that you have been maintaining the field. How long do you plan to maintain it as the baseball field? Will you still receive visitors next summer? We are planning to visit Sioux City next summer for the anniversary of the crash and would love to stop and visit the field.

Matt was 12 and loved baseball. So do I, as my father before me did. I've always coached Matt's team. For the past 6 years we have had a great time enjoying each other and baseball.

As you may know the plane crashed in an Iowa corn field. I found the whole idea very ironic; the story of an Iowa corn farmer who plows up his corn field to make a baseball field where dreams come true and my son, who loved baseball, dying in an Iowa corn field. My dreams came to an end.

When I was in Sioux City after the crash, I stayed at Briar Cliff College. From my room the most prominent object in the landscape was a baseball field. I could not stop thinking about the movie, the crash and a corn field in Iowa. There was message there.

When I read the article last evening I knew I had to visit the "field." Please let me know of your plans for the field. I hope I will have the chance to walk with my son one more time.

A single thought, by a writer living in Canada, became a dream inspiring millions, and giving comfort to a family in Bethel Park, Pa. Thus, the power of a dream.

PETER: Jim and Cindy Bohn honored me by allowing me to join them on the field in July of 1990. It was a beautiful, healing day. For me, it was a dream come true. And the dream continues.

When people say to me:
"How do you do
so many things?"
I often answer them,
without meaning
to be cruel:
"How do you do so little?"
It seems to me that people
have vast potential.
Most people can do
extraordinary things
if they have the confidence
or take the risks.
Yet most people don't.
They sit in front of the telly
and treat life as if it goes on
forever.

PHILIP ADAMS

The Thought-Feeling-Action Pyramid

Successful achievement requires the use and coordination of three things—thoughts, feelings and actions. They form the three sides of a triangle—a pyramid.

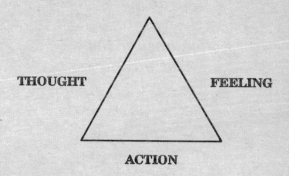

Like a stool that requires a minimum of three legs for stability, ongoing accomplishment requires thoughts, feelings and actions for success.

Thoughts spark the process, get it going. **Feelings** keep the thoughts alive, encourage more thoughts, and get the body moving. **Action** is important to accomplish the physical tasks necessary for achievement.

Without all three, the pyramid collapses. If you have a project—a thought or a dream—that doesn't seem to be "making it," perhaps one (or more) of the sides of your pyramid is in need of some work. (HINT: It's often in the area of action that people fail themselves.)

We'll be suggesting ways to strengthen and enliven thoughts, feelings and actions as we continue.

To change one's life:

- *Start immediately.*

- *Do it flamboyantly.*

- *No exceptions.*

WILLIAM JAMES

Commitment

One of the most powerful tools in the achievement toolkit is the combination of commitment with action.

W. H. Murray, in *The Scottish Himalayan Expedition,* explained it thus:

> Until one is committed, there is hesitancy, the chance to draw back, always ineffectiveness. Concerning all acts of initiative (and creation) there is one elementary truth, the ignorance of which kills countless ideas and splendid plans: that *the moment one definitely commits oneself, then Providence moves too.* All sorts of things occur to help one that would never otherwise have occurred. A whole stream of events issues from the decision, raising in one's favor all manner of unforeseen incidents and meetings and material assistance, which no man could have dreamed would have come his way. I have learned a deep respect for one of Goethe's couplets:
>
> > *Whatever you can do,*
> > *or dream you can, begin it.*
> > *Boldness has genius,*
> > *power and magic in it.*

When you're so committed to something you *know* it's going to happen, you act as though it's going to happen. That action is a powerful affirmation.

If you sit back and *say* you're committed, but wait for conclusive external proof before you act, little is likely to happen. It's called "playing it safe." We don't recommend that game. Not only is it ineffective and self-hurtful, it's already being played by people who are absolute *masters* at it. The field is overcrowded. You'll have to study long and hard to beat them at that game.

*The great aim of education
is not knowledge but action.*

HERBERT SPENCER

Be bold. Commit and act. The degree of your action can indicate the depth of your commitment. It can also determine the measure of response you'll get from your environment. If you tell friends, "I'm going to visit Hawaii, someday," they'll probably say, "That's nice."

If you tell them, however, while heading for the door, a suitcase in your hand and a nonrefundable ticket in the pocket of your funny-looking flowered shirt, your friends are more likely to say, "Can we drive you to the airport? Do you need anything? Can we help you carry your lei?"

What is your purpose? Commit to it. What experiences do you want? Commit to giving yourself those experiences regularly. Look at your top-ten list. Commit to each of them.

You are, in fact, not committing to any *project*. You are committing to yourself.

*Never esteem anything as of
advantage to you that will
make you break your word
or lose your self-respect.*

MARCUS AURELIUS ANTONINUS

121-180 A.D.

Your Word and How to Keep It

The agreements we make are always made with ourselves—and sometimes they include other people. In that sense, they are like relationships—all our relationships are with ourselves, and sometimes they include other people.

Your word is one of the most precious things you own. Do not give it lightly. Once given, do everything within your power not to break it. A broken word, like a broken cup, cannot hold very much for very long.

Does *one* broken agreement matter? One broken agreement is like a grain of sand. To a lake, one grain of sand is nothing. Gather enough grains of sand, however, and a lake becomes a swamp. Add enough more, and it becomes a bog. (Ever feel bogged down?) Add enough more, and it becomes a desert. (Did you ever feel barren inside? Did you ever plant a dream and wonder why it did not grow?)

No, one grain of sand doesn't much matter (unless, of course, the winds of fate blow it back in your eye). Gather enough grains, collected day after day for a lifetime, and the effectiveness of one's actions might be limited to sandbagging.

(If you found that last analogy heavy-handed, you should see the ones we discarded: your life might not mature beyond the sandbox; you may find yourself caught in a sand trap; if you break agreements with others, expect to get sandblasted; if you don't keep written agreements, they could turn into sandpaper; if you learn to swiftly sidestep agreements, you'll have quicksand; you may be visited by a wicked sand witch—they went on and on.)

Most of us *(we* certainly can) look back on a seemingly endless trail of broken agreements. That's a lot of sand. Is it, then, hopeless? Not at all. Declare your past broken agreements a *beach,* and get on with your life. (The techniques given in the chapters *For Giving* and *For Getting* are especially useful, as is the exercise in *Heal the Past.)*

*I phoned my dad to tell him
I had stopped smoking.
He called me a quitter.*

STEVEN PEARL

What does "keep" your word really mean? It means keep as in, "May the good Lord bless and keep you till we meet again." It means keep as in, "I will keep pure and holy my life and art" (Hippocrates – Physician's Oath). As in, "Keep thy friend" (Shakespeare); as in "And virtue, through its rays, will keep we warm" (John Dryden); as in "Put your trust in God, my boys, and keep your powder dry!" (Valentine Blacker). Keep as in, "Keep a green tree in your heart and perhaps the singing bird will come" (Chinese proverb).

If our word is so important, what (or who) would keep us from keeping it? Once again, we present a familiar cast of characters: rebels, unconsciousness, comfort junkies and approval seekers. (By the way, don't get too down on this unworthiness tribe; the Master Teachers employ them as Master Testers. They're friends, too.)

Rebels will break a rule just because it's a rule. "Rules are for fools!" they claim. They consider agreements of any kind—including ones they make, involving things they want to do—as rules. They claim they have no firm commitments in life—only options.

Unconsciousness uses the excuse, "I forgot!" whenever an agreement is broken (which is often). If they genuinely *did* forget, they consider that a sufficient explanation. When asked, "Why didn't you write it down," the unconscious may say, "I meant to, but I forgot." They misplaced their datebook long ago. How long ago? You know the answer to that one.

Comfort Junkies will keep agreements—if they want to at the moment. If it means doing something uncomfortable, however, they don't do it. This is most of the time. To make an agreement is easy. (It's less uncomfortable than saying no.) To actually *do* something when the time arrives is not comfortable. Calling and saying they won't be there is uncomfortable, too, so they avoid the whole situation.

Approval Seekers will agree to do something because, when they do, they get approval. Their schedules become hopelessly overcrowded, making the keeping of all those conflicting agreements impossible. Their reasons for

*One must have
a good memory
to be able to keep
the promises one makes.*

FRIEDRICH WILHELM NIETZSCHE

1878 (as near as we can remember)

breaking agreements are excellent ones, however—visiting the sick, feeding the homeless—designed to get approval even while breaking an agreement.

How to keep agreements? A few suggestions:

1. **Make only agreements you plan to keep.** Learn to say no, or maybe, or I'll get back to you (and *do* get back to them). If you don't want to do whatever it is you're agreeing to now, you probably won't want to do it when the time comes, so make your "no" known.

2. **Make every agreement important.** With each agreement, you give your word. Keep it sacred. Some play the game, "This agreement is more important than that agreement." In terms of ramifications "out there," that may be true, but inside yourself, each time you break your word, no matter how seemingly trivial the agreement, it costs.

3. **Keep the agreements you've made.** Even if keeping an agreement is uncomfortable, outrageously expensive, or in some way seemingly prohibitive—keep it anyway. Doing this may show you—experientially—the wisdom of suggestion #1. Slip-sliding out of agreements at the last minute will only show you that you know how to slip-slide out of agreements at the last minute. Most of us already know how to do that fairly well.

4. **Write agreements down.** Keep a calendar or datebook. Record your agreements. Review the calendar at least once a day.

5. **Communicate.** If a conflict arises and you may have to rearrange an agreement, communicate as soon as you discover the conflict. There are at least two ways to reschedule an agreement: "Something more important than keeping my agreement with you has come up, so let's reschedule it," or, "We have an agreement, and I'm willing to keep it, but I'd really appreciate it if we could move it to another time because something important has just come up." Which do you suppose is more accountable, courteous and recommended? (By the way, if you use the second

*His word burned
like a lamp.*

ECCLESIASTICUS

48:1

approach, don't do it as a technique—mean it. If they say, "I want you to keep your agreement anyway," be prepared to keep it.)

When you lovingly keep your word—keep it safe, keep it strong, keep it true—you will know the power of it. When you lend it to a cause—especially one of your own choosing—its effect will be powerful. Its effect will be known.

*For the very true
beginning of wisdom
is the desire of discipline;
and the care of discipline
is love.*

WISDOM OF SOLOMON 6:17

Discipline

Most of us associate the word discipline with punishment of a precise and exacting nature—fourth-grade teachers and the military are notorious for discipline. To call someone a disciplinarian is seldom a compliment.

To call someone Machiavellian is usually not nice, either. Maybe it was Machiavelli who gave discipline a bad name. In 1532 he wrote, "A prince should therefore have no other aim or thought but war and discipline, for that is the only art that is necessary to one who commands."

The word discipline, however, comes from two very nice words: *discipulus*, meaning pupil, and *discere*, to learn. Discipline, then, is the devotion of a disciple toward his or her learning.

We like to think of discipline not as what you must do without (the austerity school of thought), but as keeping your attention focused clearly on that which you want.

When your attention is focused on what you want, the emotions and body tend to follow. Our attention is like a flashlight beam in a dark room. What we focus the beam on, we feel (good or bad) things about, and then move our body accordingly. As Schiller wrote in 1799, "The eye sees the open heaven, / The heart is intoxicated with bliss."

For example, are you content reading this book? If so, that's the thing to focus on. You could, if you wanted to feel deprived, think about *everything else in the entire world* you *could* be doing *right now* except that you are *sacrificing all those incredible things* to sit here and read this book. But this book is supposed to be *good for you,* so keep sitting here reading it, *no matter how much you want to do all those other wonderful things.*

This is how many people view discipline. Our suggestion? Focus on where you're going. If what you're doing at the moment is not entirely pleasing (we don't mean *this* moment with *this* book, of course; we mean *some other* moment when you're *not* reading this book), ask yourself, "Does it lead to something that is pleasing?" If yes, that's the thing to focus on. If no, do something else. That's being a disciple.

Beaver: Gee, there's something wrong with just about everything, isn't there Dad?

Ward: Just about, Beav.

Positive Focusing

Ever wonder why it's so difficult to keep negative thoughts out of your mind for any period of time? Ever berate yourself for not being able to hold a more positive thought longer? There's no need for self-reproach; the odds are so stacked against us, the fact that we have *any* positive thought *at all* is something of a miracle.

Here's what we're up against:

1. **The Fight or Flight Response.** This is an in-built, physiological response to danger. When danger is perceived (not actually happening, mind you, just *perceived)* the body reacts. It calls an All Alert and prepares to either fight or flee *for its life*. This was a very handy human response for millions of years, but today, for most of us, it's counterproductive. (If you are a policeperson, a firefighter, or make your living as a contestant on television game shows, the Fight or Flight Response may still come in handy.) Part of the Fight or Flight Response is focusing the mind on *what's wrong* in the environment. This was very helpful in the days when humans had to find the saber-tooth tiger before the tiger found the human. Today, this intense, life-or-death searching for "What's wrong?" usually unearths something that isn't right. (There's always *something* that's "not right.") That "something" may trigger another round of the Fight or Flight Response. The truly bad news? All of this is *completely* automatic.

2. **Childhood programming.** As we've mentioned before, our parents, for the most part, trained us by telling us what *not* to do. All the things we did correctly—and there were many—were quickly accepted (and then expected) as "normal" behavior. Our occasional departures from their Ideal Child Behavior Matrix? The boom lowered. (You can skip this point if your parents were the kind who smiled and said, "Isn't that sweet? What remarkable individuality you're showing, dear, by

*Nobody, as long as he
moves about among the
chaotic currents of life,
is without trouble.*

CARL JUNG

pouring honey on the cat!") We were, quite a lot of the time, trained to look for the *bad* so that we would *not* do it. Is it any wonder, even today, we sometimes find ourselves unconsciously scanning the environment, looking for bad things not to do?

3. **The general negativity around us.** We turn on the news, and what's the news? *Bad* news. We pick up the newspaper and what do we read? News of fresh disasters. Commercials warn us of bad breath, body order, constipation, how it feels when a sesame seed gets under dentures. The favorite conversation? Gossip. The favorite activity? Complaining. Between 4:00 and 7:00, in cocktail lounges all over town, convenes the daily meeting of the Ain't-It-Awful Club. For the price of a drink (and you get two-for-one), you can tell your day's troubles to a stranger—providing you are willing to listen for an equal length of time. For some unknown reason, this is called The Happy Hour.

4. **Everything's falling apart (entropy).** How do you like this entropy law? Everything is in a state of deterioration. Leave something alone, and it rots. We know that, but do we need a mathematical formula to tell us how fast? Entropy comes from a Greek word meaning transformation. What they really mean is that everything is transforming into something *worse*.

All of these things will, naturally, lead to negative thoughts. *No big deal.* Really. Let them drift through your mind like leaves on a patio. There's no need to resist them, hold onto any of them, or entertain them (we're talking about thoughts here, not leaves).

The thing to be concerned with is your *focus*. Where—in the big picture of things—are you putting your attention? If you're focused on your *goal*, you can have any number of positive and negative thoughts along the way. (And probably will.)

It's a journey. As long as you keep moving toward your destination, you're doing fine. It's when you stop moving, or are not moving toward your destination, that some course correction is in order.

*The only reason
I would take up jogging is
so that I could hear
heavy breathing again.*

ERMA BOMBECK

Those who enjoy being on the train, and those who do not enjoy being on the train, get to the same destination at the same time. Yes, there are things you can do to enjoy the train more. Lots of techniques for this are given in the next section (Part Five). For now, however, know that being on the train that's going in the direction of your choice is all it takes.

Naturally, the more positive thoughts you have, the more positive you'll feel. If you want to feel happy, think about happy things. An unending stream of "happy thoughts" is not, however, necessary to reach your goal. *Motion* and *direction* are.

The words "I am..."
are potent words;
be careful what
you hitch them to.
The thing you're claiming
has a way of reaching back
and claiming you.

A. L. KITSELMAN

Affirmations

"Affirmation" means to make firm, solid, more real. Thoughts—not very solid—when repeated over and over, become more and more firm. They become feelings, behaviors, experiences and things. What we think about, we can become.

We affirm all the time. Sometimes we affirm negative things; sometimes we affirm positive things. In the words of Henry Ford, "If you think you can do a thing, or think you can't do a thing; you're right."

. We, of course, are going to suggest that you consciously affirm the positive. Many of us already have the unconscious habit of affirming the negative. To change that, we quote Johnny Mercer, "You've got to accentuate the positive, eliminate the negative, latch onto the affirmative."

Affirmations usually begin with "I am..." "I am a happy, healthy, wealthy person." "I am joyful no matter what is happening around me." "I am loving and kind." If you're affirming for material things, it's a good idea to start even those with "I am..." "I am enjoying my new house." "I am creative and content in my new career."

Affirmations are best in the present tense. "I want a new car," affirms what? *Wanting* a new car. If what you want is *wanting* a new car, then that's a good affirmation. What you probably want, however, is the *car.* "I am safely and happily enjoying my beautiful new car." Affirm as though you already have what you want, even though you don't yet have it. (The operative word is "yet.")

No matter how "impossible" something may seem, put it into an affirmation form and give it a try. Say it, out loud, at least 100 times before you decide how "impossible" something might be. After 100 repetitions, you may find yourself quite comfortable with the idea.

You can write affirmations on paper and put them in places you will see them—on the bathroom mirror, refrigerator, next to your bed, on the car dashboard. You can also record them on endless-loop cassette tapes and play them in the background all day (and night) long.

I'd love to see
Christ come back to
crush the spirit of hate
and make men
put down their guns.
I'd also like just one more
hit single.

TINY TIM

A powerful technique is to say your affirmation while looking into your eyes in a mirror. All your limitations about the thing you're affirming are likely to surface, but persevere. Outlast the negative voices and doubting feelings. Plant the seed of your affirmation deep.

You can use affirmations written by other people, but remember that you are perfectly capable of creating your own. If you don't think so, start with the affirmation, "I am enjoying the success of the wonderful affirmations I create for myself." That should be the last affirmation anyone needs to write for you. (And you probably could have created a better one than *that*.)

Your purpose is already an affirmation. Say it to yourself often. Create affirmations for each of the experiences you want. They can be very simple: "I am content." "I am joyful and calm in the peace of my mind." "I am feeling love." "I am strong and powerful." Also, write several affirmations for each item on your top-ten list.

Affirmations work if you use them. The more you use them, the more they work. They can be used anywhere, anytime, while doing almost anything.

It's a good idea (a very good idea) to end all your affirmations with "...this or something better, for the highest good of all concerned."

The "...this or something better..." lets ten million come in when you merely asked for a million, and "...for the highest good of all concerned," assures that your affirmation is fulfilled in a way that's best for everyone.

Learn to automatically turn all your wishes and wants into affirmations. Then start catching your negative thoughts, switching them around, and making affirmations out of them. By only slightly revising the negative chatter (changing "can't" to "can," "won't" to "will," "hate" to "love," etc.), you can turn all those formerly limiting voices into a staff of in-house affirmation writers.

Here are a few to get you started, but this is a very brief list.

Affirmation of life
is the spiritual act
by which man ceases
to live unreflectively
and begins to devote himself
to his life with reverence
in order to raise it
to its true value.
To affirm life is to deepen,
to make more inward,
and to exalt the will to live.

ALBERT SCHWEITZER

- "I am feeling warm and loving toward myself."
- "I am worthy of all the good in my life."
- "I am one with the universe, and I have more than I need."
- "I am happy that I always do the best I can with what I know and always use everything for my advancement."
- "I am forgiving myself unconditionally."
- "I am grateful for my life."
- "I am loving and accepting myself and others."
- "I am treating all problems as opportunities to grow in wisdom and love."
- "I am relaxed, trusting in a higher plan that's unfolding for me."
- "I am automatically and joyfully focusing on the positive."
- "I am giving myself permission to live, love and laugh."
- "I am creating and singing affirmations to create a joyful, abundant, fulfilling life."
- ...this or something better for the highest good of all concerned.

*It's no good running
a pig farm badly for
thirty years while saying,
"Really I was meant to be
a ballet dancer."
By that time,
pigs will be your style.*

QUENTIN CRISP

Effectiveness vs. Efficiency

The best comparison between effectiveness and efficiency we've heard is this: Efficiency is getting the job done *right*. Effectiveness is getting the *right job done*.

People who excel in life—the so-called "winners"—don't do twice as much or five times as much or a hundred times as much as "average" people. Winners, it has been shown, only do a few percentage points more than everybody else.

The winner of a two-hour marathon need only be a few seconds ahead of all the other runners to win. First, second and third place winners can all come in within a minute of each other. The 20,000 other runners are simply numbers.

In business, the winners often make only five more phone calls per day than average, or read five more journals per month, or get five more good ideas per year.

But it's not *volume* or *speed* we're necessarily talking about. In athletic competition, as in life, it's not *how many* events you win, but *which ones* that determine the champions.

Some explain this with the 80/20 theory: 80% of your effort produces 20% of your results, and 20% of your effort produces 80% of your results.

The theory claims that you spend 80% of your time wearing 20% of your clothes, and 20% of your time wearing 80% of your clothes; you spend 80% of your time with 20% of your friends, and 20% of your time with 80% of your friends; you spend 20% of your career resources producing 80% of your results, and 80% of your resources producing 20% of your results; and so on.

These aren't precise figures, of course. They do, however, show that *effort* and *results* are not necessarily in direct proportion—not even close, in fact.

If the 80/20 theory is even partially true, imagine what would happen if you started taking time and resources from the less effective 80% activities and moved

*I take my children
everywhere, but they always
find their way back home.*

ROBERT ORBEN

them to the highly effective 20% things. One percent more *effective* action would produce 5% more results.

How can you tell the 80% from the 20%? Watch. Look. Listen. Listen, for example, to Rudyard Kipling's nursery rhyme: "I keep six honest serving men / (They taught me all I knew); / Their names are What and Why and When / And How and Where and Who." Keep track of what you do and the results it produces.

You'll notice patterns emerging. "I spend as much time doing A as doing B, but B produces twice as many results." When you notice that, take a little time from A and give it to B. See what happens. Yes, you will probably get less from A, but do you get proportionately more from B?

Here's our nursery rhyme for today (if it's good enough for Rudyard Kipling…): "Life's experiments are great fun. / This is but another one."

*While one person hesitates
because he feels inferior,
the other is busy
making mistakes and
becoming superior.*

HENRY C. LINK

It's Not that People Plan to Fail, They Just Fail to Plan

Here is the truth about making a plan: It never works. If, however, you *do* make a plan, the chances of getting what you want significantly increase.

When we say, "plans never work," what do we mean? Let's say you made a plan to do something. You broke your goal into action steps, and estimated the approximate amount of time each step would take. The plan was for step A to take one week, step B to take two weeks, step C to take one week, step D to take a month, and step E to take a day. This would lead you to F, which is what you want.

When you get to F, however, you may look back on your original plan with amusement: Almost nothing went "according to plan." Step A took only a day. Step B took a week. Step C, as it turned out, had five subsets to it, taking two weeks *each*. When you got to step D, you discovered that nobody did step D anymore. Step E took ten minutes.

Without the faulty plan, however, you might never have ventured forth to learn all you needed to know to get to F. F is where you wanted to go; F is where you got. You just didn't get there the way you had planned. So, even though we know it's probably not going to be accurate, we're suggesting you make a plan anyway.

If you don't already have one, get a date book of some kind with room for daily planning. Then start laying out your step-by-step progression for each of your top-ten list. We strongly suggest you plan *at least* one activity from *each* of your top ten *each* week.

Why?

Ready for a hard truth? *If you're not actively involved in getting what you want, you don't really want it.*

People kid themselves for years—decades, sometimes—with a goal that, in fact, they don't really want. How do we know they didn't want it? Because they never really did anything to get it. If they really wanted it, we

*Zeus does not bring all
men's plans to fulfillment.*

HOMER

figure, they would have, over the years, consistently done something to get it. (We are a pragmatic pair.)

People look back and say, "I coulda been..." this, or "I coulda had..." that. Maybe, but they also "coulda" done more to obtain it. We don't want you to face a case of the coulda's. Please do something about each of your top-ten list every week.

After a few months of doing something each week, you may discover you don't want it after all. Without the action, however, you might not have known it. If you decide you don't want it, a slot in your top-ten list has just opened up.

If you're scheduling things *not* on your top-ten list, and finding you "don't have time" for things on your top-ten list, we suggest you either (A) rearrange your top-ten list, or (B) rearrange your schedule.

Break each of your top-ten goals into *next doable steps*. A doable step is something you can actually do. "Learn to use a computer," is too vague. "Call friends who have a computer and ask the best way to learn to use a computer," is a doable step. You can schedule that one—give it a date, time and duration. (April 16, 4:00 p.m., two hours.) If you can't assign it a date, time and duration, there's probably a more doable next doable step available.

Then start writing these steps in your date book. Schedule your time. Budget your time as you would budget your money. Use a pencil, as you're apt to make changes, but do commit to the steps you put in your book. Be flexible, of course. This is meant to be a spur to action, not a hog-tie.

For the next few weeks, plan hour by hour. The next month, day by day. The months after that, week by week. When you project a project to completion, pick another and start scheduling that.

Sitting with the days of your life before you—all the time you have to spend on *everything*—and allocating what will receive which portion of time when, can be confusing, exhilarating, painful, exciting, fearful—and a dozen other things—all at once.

*We can act
<u>as if</u> there were a God;
feel <u>as if</u> we were free;
consider Nature <u>as if</u> she
were full of special designs;
lay plans <u>as if</u> we were to be
immortal; and we find then
that these words do make a
genuine difference in
our moral life.*

WILLIAM JAMES

But please do it. One thing's for sure: you'll spend that time doing *something*. The only question is: do you want to control your time, or do you want your time to control you? When you don't take charge, time, by default, takes over.

(Insight Consulting Group teaches an excellent course called Managing Accelerated Productivity. It helps in deciding what you want and offers specific techniques on how to go about getting it. It's taught in many cities in the U.S. and around the world. For more information, please write ICG, 2101 Wilshire Blvd., Santa Monica, California 90403, or call 213-829-2100.)

You said, "but."
I've put my finger
on the whole trouble.
You're a "but" man.
Don't say, "but."
That little word "but"
is the difference between
success and failure.
Henry Ford said,
"I'm going to
invent the automobile,"
and Arthur T. Flanken said,
"But..."

SGT. ERNIE BILKO
THE PHIL SILVERS SHOW

Get Off Your Buts!

You know what life is for; you know what your limitations are; you know the true identity of your Master Teachers; you have tools, tools and more tools; you know what you want; you've planned it out—all right—ready, set...

Do it!

When joined together, these can be two of the most frightening words in the English language. People know what they want; they know what to do to get it; they have the time, energy and opportunity; and then comes the magic words, *do it,* and panic descends.

The unworthiness warriors march out in full regalia. Rebellion says, "But why should I do it *their* way? I'll do it *my way* in *my own time.*" Unconsciousness stumbles forward and says, "But this is all too much to keep track of." The approval seeker compliments us on the book's cover, but claims to be already overcommitted.

In situations of action vs. status quo, however, one of the unworthiness tribe stands head and shoulders above the rest: comfort junkies.

Consider this: people have precisely what they want in their lives—not what they *think* they want, but what they *actually want.*

What we have is based upon moment-to-moment choices of what we *do.* In each of those moments, we choose. We either take a risk and move toward what we want, or we play it safe and choose comfort.

Most of the people, most of the time, choose comfort. In the end, people either have excuses or experiences; reasons or results; buts or brilliance; they either have what they wanted, or they have a detailed list of all the rational reasons why not. (Remember: rationalize = rational lies.)

Almost all excuses and reasons are motivated by fear—fear of fatigue, fear of not doing it perfectly, fear of looking foolish, fear of mistakes, fear of losing, fear of

*Victory belongs to
the most persevering.*

NAPOLEON

being let down, fear of facing unworthiness, fear of getting angry; in short, fear that we might be uncomfortable.

We tell ourselves, "I won't do this now, I'm too tired. *But,* I'll do it tomorrow when I can make a fresh start." The next morning, "I'm not in the mood. *But* I'll do it this afternoon." Come afternoon, there's some other "important" activity. It's postponed till evening, when friends just happen to stop over, *but* everything is put off until the following morning—*but* again.

These reasons, by the way, are not always negative in nature. Sometimes they are the most wonderful, positive "opportunities": a party, a trip, a dinner, friends, relationships, "easy money," and so on.

We call them all—positive or negative—the same thing: distractions. If they're not definite steps on the way to your goals, they're distractions.

(Not that there's no room for fun, joy and play. Far from it: we would consider a list of goals rather feeble that didn't have one of those in at least the top five.)

When a distraction arises, ask yourself: would you rather have the distraction, or would you rather have your goal? It's tough to see it that way, because the goal of, say, writing a book may mean an entire evening spent researching a dull but important detail. This research cannot compare to the fun of the party to which you've just been invited.

The accurate question to ask yourself is: which is more important, the party or the book? *Not:* which is more appealing at this moment, the party or the dull research? After a thousand choices—distraction vs. work—you will have either (A) an extensive collection of party favors, or (B) a book.

These choices are made daily, hourly, moment by moment.

If you want to achieve more, declare your reasons unreasonable, your excuses inexcusable—and get off your buts!

*In Endymion, I leaped
headlong into the sea,
and thereby have become
better acquainted with the
soundings, the quicksands,
and the rocks, than if I had
stayed upon the green shore,
and piped a silly pipe,
and took tea and
comfortable advice.*

JOHN KEATS

1818

The Comfort Zone

We all live within an area called the comfort zone. It's the arena of activities we have done often enough to feel comfortable doing them. For most of us, this includes walking, talking, driving, spending time with certain friends, making money in certain ways—all those once-difficult and fearful things that we now find easy and comfortable.

You can imagine the comfort zone as a circle: Inside the circle are those things we are comfortable doing; outside is everything else. The wall of the circle is not, alas, a wall of protection. It is a wall of fear; a wall of limitation.

The *illusion* is that the wall keeps us from bad things and keeps bad things from us. In reality, the bad things get in just fine (perhaps you've noticed). In reality, too, the wall often prevents us from getting what we want.

When we do something new, something different, we push against the parameters of our comfort zone. If we do the new thing often enough, we overcome the fear, and our comfort zone expands. If we back off and honor the "need" to be comfortable, our comfort zone shrinks. It's a dynamic, living thing, always expanding or contracting.

When it expands in one area, it expands in other areas as well. When we succeed at something, our confidence and self-esteem increases, and we take that confidence and self-esteem with us into other endeavors.

When we "give in" to our comfort zone, the zone contracts. Our belief that we "aren't strong enough," "can't do it" and are, basically, "not good enough," often prevents us from even *thinking* about approaching "the zone" again for some time.

For some, the comfort zone shrinks to the size of their apartment: they never leave home without anxiety; some people never leave home at all. They sit and watch the news on TV. This certainly supports the notion that it's a hostile, dangerous place out there, and it's better to stay home.

*Life is either
a daring adventure
or nothing.
Security does not exist in nature,
nor do the children of men
as a whole experience it.
Avoiding danger is no safer
in the long run than exposure.*

HELEN KELLER

Push on—keep moving.

THOMAS MORTON
1797

For a few, the comfort zone shrinks to a space smaller than their own body. We've all probably seen or heard about institutionalized people who are afraid to move any part of their body in any way. That is when the comfort zone "wins" its greatest victory.

That and suicide. The "it" some people refer to who "just can't take it anymore" is the need to *constantly* be confronting the comfort zone just to keep it at bay.

Here is one of the great ironies of life: Those who are doing what they want to do and are consciously expanding their comfort zone at every opportunity *experience* no more fear than people who are passively trying to keep life "as comfortable as possible."

Fear is a part of life. Some people feel fear when they press against their comfort zone and make it larger. Other people feel fear when they even *think* they *might* do something that gets them even *close* to the (evershrinking, in their case) comfort zone. *Both feel the same fear.*

In fact, the person in the shrinking comfort zone probably feels more fear. They not only feel fear, they also feel the fear of feeling fear; and the fear of the fear of feeling fear; and on and on. The person who develops the habit of moving through fear when it appears, feels it only once. It's the old, "A coward dies a thousand deaths, a brave man dies but one," idea. (Earlier, of course, we learned how to *enjoy* fear—but that's another lesson.)

Some people don't just honor their comfort zone, they *worship* it. When they feel fear, they think it is God saying to them, personally and directly, "Don't do this." Some have, in fact, found scriptural references to support their inaction. Not doing new things becomes a matter of *morality*. Those pagans who "don't listen to God" and have the audacity to try new things are not only damned, they should be locked up.

For these dear souls, we have two quotes, "And the angel said unto them, Fear not: for, behold, I bring you good tidings of great joy, which shall be to all people." (Luke 2:10). The shepherds who were afraid to "try something new" (listening to an angel in a field) never made it to the manger. And then there's 1 John 4:18, "There is no

*A coward dies
a hundred deaths,
a brave man only once...
But then, once is enough,
isn't it?*

JUDGE HARRY STONE

fear in love; but perfect love casteth out fear." This is our favorite method of expanding the comfort zone: Love it all.

In the air conditioning trade, "the comfort zone" is the range of temperatures on the thermostat (usually around 72 degrees) in which neither heating nor air conditioning is needed. It's also called "the dead zone."

That's the end result of honoring the comfort zone too much, too often: a sense of deadness; a feeling of being trapped in a life not of our desiring, doing things not of our choosing, spending time with people not of our liking.

The answer to all of this? Do it. Feel the fear, and do it anyway. Physically move to accomplish those things you choose. Eventually, learn to make friends with the Master Teacher fear.

Learn to love it all.

(This seems the ideal opportunity to recommend our book *DO IT! Let's Get Off Our Buts.* At your local bookstore, or call 1-800-LIFE-101.)

Many a time
we've been down to
our last piece of fatback.
And I'd say,
"Should we eat it,
or render it down for soap?"
Your Uncle Jed would say,
"Render it down.
God will provide food
for us poor folks,
but we gotta
do our own washin'."

GRANNY
THE BEVERLY HILLBILLIES

Money

We have so many conflicting beliefs about money in our culture. Some are uplifting, some are "downpushing." It's little wonder that the way most people feel about money is simply *confused*.

If you want more money, here's how to get it:

1. Reduce the number of limiting beliefs you have about money.

2. Increase the positive beliefs you hold.

3. Do what it takes to get money.

Money is simply a symbol of energy. We use money so that, as authors, we don't have to carry books with us and trade them for whatever it is we want. ("How many scoops of vanilla fudge almond can I get for a book about life?")

It's a convenience. Can you imagine the chaos if you had to trade your marketable skills for the things you needed? Can you imagine a conversation between a secretary and the owner of a plum tree?

"I'd like some plums."

"What do you have to trade?"

"I can type a letter. I'll type a letter for a dozen plums."

"I don't have any letters."

"Well, then I'll type one for you."

"I don't need any letters. What else you got?"

"I can Xerox."

"I don't have any letters. I don't have anything to Xerox."

"I can send a fax."

"Facts about what?"

"No, fax. Facsimile. You use it to send letters."

"How many times do I have to tell you? I don't *have* any letters."

"What do you want?"

From birth to age 18,
a girl needs good parents,
from 18 to 35
she needs good looks,
from 35 to 55
she needs
a good personality,
and from 55 on
she needs cash.

SOPHIE TUCKER

"I want a chicken."

"I don't have a chicken."

"Do you have a duck?"

"No."

"A goose?"

"I don't have any poultry of any kind."

"Do you have a color TV?"

"Yes."

"I'll trade you a dozen plums for a color TV."

"That's not a fair trade."

"All right. Two dozen plums. And a rooster."

"You have a rooster? I thought you wanted a chicken."

"The rooster wanted the chicken. I told him I'd help him out. But if I get a TV, I don't care about the rooster."

Do you see how much more cumbersome life would be if we had to barter for everything? Money is a symbol of energy. For a certain amount of energy, you are given a symbol. You can then trade that symbol for something that requires someone else's energy.

Let's look at the limiting beliefs some people have about money. None of them is true, by the way. The one you want to *prove* to us is true is the very belief you would probably do best to *dis*prove for yourself—if you want more money, that is.

To disprove any of these, all we have to do is show that they are not true for *one person*. If one person did it, you can be number two. The statement, "All birds are red," can be disproved by finding just *one* bluebird.

It takes money to make money. There are stories galore of people who started with nothing—sometimes less than nothing (they inherited debts)—and made great fortunes. It takes effectiveness and perseverance, not money, to make money.

Poor is pure. Some of the grinding poverty we have seen is hardly "pure." It's often filthy, fly-ridden and disease-laden. It doesn't seem to induce inner purity, either.

*Lack of money
is the root of all evil.*

GEORGE BERNARD SHAW

Not that there aren't pure poor people. We, however, happen to think they'd be just as pure if they were rich. We have also met some people we'd consider pure who have lots of money.

People resent rich people. Some people resent rich people, some people resent poor people, some people resent people who resent other people. Some people also *respect* rich people.

Wealthy people are snobby. We've met some down-to-earth poor people, and we've met some dirt-poor snobs, too. Some people snub others for not being "enough"—not pretty enough, not smart enough, not evolved enough. Money's just one of the things snobby people get snobbish about, regardless of income level.

It is easier for a camel to go through the eye of a needle than for a rich man to enter the kingdom of God. That's from the Bible, quoting Jesus (Matthew 19:24). Actually, it's not hard for a camel to get through the eye of the needle. We both got through. "The needle" is the name of a gate in Jerusalem. The "eye" is the small doorway in the larger gate. When the main gate was closed, the eye would open. In order for a camel to pass through the eye of the needle, the camel must (A) stand in line (when the main gate is closed and only the eye open, there tends to be a line); (B) have its cargo removed; and (C) go through on its knees (which camels have no trouble doing).

Knowing that Jesus taught in parables, what do you suppose might have been the message? In order to enter the Kingdom of God (which Jesus said was "within" [Luke 17:21]), a rich man must (A) be patient; (B) unburden himself of his cargo (he can keep it, he just can't be attached to it); and (C) be humble, or in a symbolic posture of reverence (on the knees). That makes sense to us. If you don't prefer this interpretation, there are stores for rich people that sell *great big* needles and *little teeny* stuffed camels. You can sit all day long, if you like, putting a camel through the eye of a needle.

Money is the root of all evil. Back to the Bible. (Is it any wonder this has been called the world's most misunderstood book?) This one's from 1 Timothy 6:10. The

If I were rich
I'd have
The time that I lack
To sit in the
Synagogue and pray,
And maybe have a seat
by the Eastern Wall.

And I'd discuss the
Holy Books
With the learned men
Seven hours every day.
That would be the
sweetest thing of all.

SHELDON HARNICK
FIDDLER ON THE ROOF

full sentence is, "The love of money is the root of all evil." In other translations, it reads, "The love of money is the root of *all kinds of* evil," (New International Version), and, a more accurate word in that sentence for love is "lust." The sentence then is, "Lusting after money is the root of all kinds of evil." We have no argument with that. Lusting after *anything* can be the root of all kinds of evil. Money is neither good nor evil in itself. It can be used for either, depending on the intentions of the user.

You need training and education to get money. There are many stories of people who made great fortunes, with which they endowed great educational institutions, while they themselves never graduated from elementary school. It's what you know, not the amount of time you spent in school, that determines your ability to make money.

Money can't buy me love. As a friend of ours pointed out, "Whoever wrote that doesn't know where to shop."

You can't take it with you. True, but anywhere you can't take it, you wouldn't want it anyway.

Money is too much responsibility. If you have that much money, you can hire people to shoulder the burden of all that responsibility for you.

It takes hard work to make money. It takes *smart* work to make money. (In other words, being effective, not just efficient.)

Money isn't everything. No, but it's something.

The best things in life are free. As the same friend of ours pointed out, "Whoever wrote that doesn't shop where I shop."

Money isn't spiritual or holy. And poverty is? In fact, if you had lots of money you could spend lots more time praying, meditating, buying yachts for your guru, putting a new wing on your church—whatever would help you get closer to God.

Eliminating limiting beliefs about money is a good way to get more money. Another good way is enhancing *uplifting* beliefs. Just to show you we're not the only ones

Lovey Howell: You know, I really wouldn't mind being poor, if it weren't for one thing.

Thurston Howell III: What is that, my dear?

Lovey: Poverty.

who have a high regard for money, here's what *other people* have said in praise of money:

- Money is a sweet balm. (Arabian Proverb)
- Money is a guarantee that we may have what we want in the future. Though we need nothing at the moment, it insures the possibility of satisfying a necessary desire when it arises. (Aristotle)
- Money is the sovereign queen of all delights—for her, the lawyer pleads, the soldier fights. (Richard Barnfield)
- Money is the symbol of everything that is necessary for man's well-being and happiness. Money means freedom, independence, liberty. (Edward E. Beals)
- Money is the sinews of art and literature. (Samuel Butler)
- Money is Aladdin's lamp. (Lord Byron)
- Money is the representative of a certain quantity of corn or other commodity. Its value is in the necessities of the animal man. It is so much warmth, so much bread. (Ralph Waldo Emerson)
- Money is like an arm or a leg—use it or lose it. (Henry Ford)
- Money is health, and liberty, and strength. (Charles Lamb)
- Money is the sixth sense which enables you to enjoy the other five. (Somerset Maugham)
- Money is that which brings honor, friends, conquest, and realms. (John Milton)
- Money is the only substance which can keep a cold world from nicknaming a citizen "Hey, you!" (Wilson Mizner)
- Money is the cause of good things to a good man, of evil things to a bad man. (Philo)
- Money is human happiness in the abstract. (Arthur Schopenhauer)

*A private railroad car
is not an acquired taste.
One takes to it immediately.*

ELEANOR R. BELMONT

- Money is the most important thing in the world. (George Bernard Shaw)

- Money is an article which may be used as a universal passport to everywhere except heaven, and as a universal provider for everything except happiness. (Wall Street Journal)

- Money is the root of all good. (Rudolf Wanderone)

Here are some suggestions on how to have more money:

1. Remember that money is just a *symbol* of *energy*. What you do with the energy will determine the money's effect on you and those around you.

2. Money is a method—not an intention, belief or experience. Money in and of itself will not make you happy, joyful, fulfilled, content or anything else. It will make you *rich*, but that, too, is a symbol. Money is a tool. You can build things with tools, but the tool is not the thing you want built.

3. Be open to receiving money from any source, in any amount, in any form, at any time. Learn to say, "Yes, thank you," when people offer you things that have financial value.

4. Be open to spend. Life is cycles of giving and receiving. We breathe in, we breathe out. The exhale is as important as the inhale. If we stop either inhaling or exhaling for any period of time, life becomes remarkably uncomfortable. Also, keeping the money flowing about you allows for more of the *experiences* you wanted the money for in the first place.

5. Affirm money. Use affirmations that contain the words, "money," "cash," "dollars," and so on. (As with the word "death," we seem to avoid using the word "money." If you want money, ask for money.) "I am enjoying the large sums of money that flow into my life, quickly and effortlessly, this or something better for my highest good and the highest good of all concerned."

6. Give 10% away. This is called tithing. By giving 10% away (to your church, your favorite charity,

*Money-giving is
a very good criterion
of a person's mental health.
Generous people are
rarely mentally ill people.*

DR. KARL A. MENNINGER

any cause *you* believe in), you are not only passing some energy along for good use, you are saying, "Thank you. I have more than I need." This
is a great statement of abundance, and great
statements of abundance can create greater abundance. Be a joyful giver so that you can also be a
joyful receiver.

7. Enjoy the money you have. If you think you don't
have enough to enjoy yourself now, you will probably not have enough when you have millions.
Remove the "unfun" you may have attached to
money. Take some money and do something *enjoyable*. Right now.

8. Be grateful for the money you already have.
When we were in Egypt, we stopped at a town on
the banks of the Nile. The richest man in town
had something no one else in town had. It was
this one possession that made him the richest
man in town. Everyone knew he was the richest
man in town because he had this. With great
pride he showed it to us. What do you think it
was? A TV? A dishwasher? A blender? No. The
town had no electricity. A bathtub? A sink? A toilet? No. The town had no running water. The
man was the richest man in town because he had
a cement floor. It was cracked, it was filthy, it
was falling apart, but he was proud of it because
everyone else's floor was dirt. Be grateful for the
money (and things you bought with the money)
you have.

9. We don't have a number 9, but most lists of ten
things have a number 9, so we thought this one
might as well.

10. Keep 10% of your increase as a "money magnet."
Keep it, in cash or tangible valuables. As it grows,
it attracts money to you. How? The more you
have, the less anxiety you feel about money,
therefore the more you get.

(More about all this in John-Roger's book *Wealth and
Higher Consciousness*. Available from Mandeville Press,
Box 3935, Los Angeles, CA 90051. 213-737-4055)

*A friend is a gift
you give yourself.*

ROBERT LOUIS STEVENSON

The Power of Partnership

The support you can gather from good friends, groups, and your Master Teacher is formidable. The encouragement you can give them in return (yes, even Master Teachers need a little encouragement at times) is substantial.

To use your goals and aspirations as small talk over dinner dissipates their energy. But to meet with like minds and discuss the challenges and triumphs of mastering your life; *that* has power, splendor and esteem.

- Friends are, of course, invaluable—for both creation and recreation. People who love us for what we are, not what we have done, are precious support when we're trying to do and be more.

- You can form or join a support group of like-minded people moving in a similar direction. Regular meetings at which victories are celebrated, problems solved, and new ideas brainstormed, can be unparalleled in their ability to produce ongoing results.

- Professional counselors, advisors and consultants are available—at a price of course—but the insight and wisdom they can impart in a brief session may be priceless.

- Books, tapes and courses of all kinds make you "partners" with the finest minds of all time. Just because people aren't there "in person" doesn't mean there's not a relationship between you and them. For the most part, people take the time to write a book, make a tape or teach a course because they *care*. Be the beneficiary of their knowledge, experience and caring.

- Lest we forget, you have many Master Teachers—and your own personal Master Teacher, who is always with you. Spend time in your sanctuary with your Master Teacher. Learn to listen to your Master Teacher's voice throughout the day. The dialogue between the two of you can be ongoing.

*I think and think for
months and years.
Ninety-nine times,
the conclusion is false.
The hundredth time
I am right.*

ALBERT EINSTEIN

How Much is Enough?

People often wonder: How long will this take? How much work is enough? How much affirming, planning and acting must I do to get what I want?

The answer is very simple.

When you have what you want, it was enough.

This is not the answer most people want to hear. We are so used to delivery schedules and travel timetables that pinpoint precisely when what (or we) will arrive, it's hard to accept the ancient wisdom, "It'll shine when it shines."

Sorry. That is the only answer we have. When we began working on *You Can't Afford the Luxury of a Negative Thought,* we thought it would take much longer to write than it did. When we decided to publish it as a book (it was originally designed as support material for a workshop), we thought things would go much faster than they did. Such is life.

Our estimates of time are only estimates, best guesses. Some things will happen sooner, some will happen later. If a dream is worth dreaming, it's worth living.

If your goal is not reached in the time frame you set, set a new time frame. Do what else needs to be done to get it. When you've done all that, and that's still not enough, do some more. When do you stop doing? When you've gotten what you want.

People sometimes get *so close* to their goals, then they stop. They become discouraged. It's discouraging how discouraged some people can get. When you take the "dis" off "discourage," you have what you need to press on: courage. When things don't happen "on schedule," hire a squad of cheerleaders to remind you, "Don't get pissed off, take the 'dis' off."

Do whatever it takes to achieve the results you want. Don't accept the limitations of other people who claim things are "unchangeable." If it's written in stone, bring your hammer and chisel.

When you have what you want, that was enough.

I am open to receive
With every breath I breathe.

Receiving

Some people select their goals, do the necessary work, and still don't have what they want. As we've just noted, they need to do more work, but maybe it's not external work. Maybe it's on themselves.

When we work for something, we must be open to receive it. This may seem silly, but some people have some rather definite limits on *what* they can receive and *how* they can receive it. If you try to give them a million dollars, they'll accept it, but *only if* the million dollars is in new $100 bills, and it must be delivered to the back door. At 4:15 sharp. Next Wednesday.

If we want more, it's helpful to know *how* to receive more. We receive more by saying, "Yes." If they want to give you a million dollars in pennies, take it. If they want you to pick them up, say you'll be right over. If they want to deliver it, tell 'em, "Pick your door."

Just as you have many methods and behaviors for fulfilling your desires and intentions, life has many ways to give you what you've been asking for. (Working on getting what you want is one of the sincerest forms of asking, by the way.)

Remember, too, that you are worthy of all the good that comes your way. How do we know? If you weren't worthy, it wouldn't come your way. If you want a relationship, and someone "over and above" your dreams appears on your doorstep with flowers and candy, don't say, "You must have the wrong house"—*invite them in.*

Make a new affirmation for yourself for each of your desired experiences and for each item on your top-ten list. Let each begin, "I am worthy of..." and then list the experience or thing you want. Make another affirmation that begins, "I am open to receive..." Add these to your list of affirmations, and say them often.

If you hear a knocking on the door, open it. It may be someone with flowers and candy, or it may be a lot of pennies. And it may be both.

PART FIVE

*Gladness of the heart
is the life of a man,
and the joyfulness of a man
prolongeth his days.*

ECCLESIASTICUS

30:22

PART FIVE

TO HAVE JOY AND TO HAVE IT MORE ABUNDANTLY

There is no end to joy. There is no upper limit. It can be there no matter what else you're feeling, thinking or doing.

When you think you've had all the joy you can tolerate, you've only reached *your* limit, not joy's. Use that moment to expand your limit. Don't just increase joy by a little. Double it. Then, double that. Discover that your capacity to know joy is as limitless as joy itself.

As limitless as you yourself.

The chapters in this section are shorter, more to the point. The point will always point to the same place: your heart, your loving, your happiness, your peace, your joy, you.

We'll point, and step back—letting you discover.

The human race,
to which so many
of my readers belong,
has been playing
at children's games
from the beginning,
which is a nuisance for
the few people who grow up.

G. K. CHESTERTON

1904

Grow Up!

Ever watch anyone have a temper tantrum? Or go on and on about how unfairly the world treated them? Or cry over the loss of someone they didn't much like anyway? Or watch a fit of jealousy, pettiness or vindictiveness?

On those occasions, didn't you want to quote Joan Rivers: *"Grow up!"*

We're not talking about the child*like* qualities—joy, playfulness, spontaneity—we're talking about the child*ish* traits—spoiled, petulant, fatuous, idiotic, infantile, inconsiderate.

This sort of immaturity hurts and offends not just those around us, it hurts and offends *ourselves*. Even while we're doing it, we know, "This isn't right." Even through the anger, fear and separation, we know, "This isn't necessary."

And it's not. It's time to mature, to ripen, to grow up.

*I don't have
a warm personal enemy left.
They've all died off.
I miss them terribly
because
they helped define me.*

CLAIRE BOOTH LUCE

Heal the Past

The parts of the past that hurt are its memories. We remember the pain and horror of what happened, and we hurt again. Fortunately, we can heal the memories of the past.

One technique for doing this is to go into your sanctuary (remembering to let the light at your entryway surround, fill, protect, bless and heal you for your highest good), sit in front of the Video Screen, and, on the Screen, watch the memory that is causing the pain. The "halo" around the screen is dark. Let the memory play itself out. (If the images are difficult, you might ask your Master Teacher to join you. Master Teachers are great for holding hands, giving comfort and encouraging courage. As one once said, "I'm at my best when you're at your worst.")

Then let the image fade. See the white light around the screen glow brightly. Then see the same scene the way you wanted it to be. What do you wish had happened? See it. What do you wish you had said? Hear yourself saying it. How do you wish others had responded? See them responding that way. What would you like to have felt? Feel that.

Replacing a negative memory with a positive one heals it.

You can also use your Health Center. Perhaps there is a special memory-healing device, or magic elixir, or a Master with a touch—or maybe just a look—that heals. Whatever you wish medical science had that would heal the past, imagine it in your Health Center, and use it.

If the hurt involves other people, you can invite them to visit your sanctuary. Under the guidance and protection of your Master Teacher, you can tell them whatever it is you want them to know, forgive them (and yourself), and then let them go into that pure, white light of the People Mover.

Healing of memories takes time, and no small amount of courage, but the results are worthy of the effort.

Of one thing I am certain,
the body is not
the measure of healing
—peace is the measure.

GEORGE MELTON

Health is the state about which
medicine has nothing to say.

W. H. AUDEN

Health

Health is more than just the absence of illness. Health is the presence of aliveness, energy, joy.

By constantly focusing on eliminating illness, few of us learn how to enhance health—or even that such a thing is possible. It is.

You don't have to be sick to get better.

Health is not just for the body. Health includes the mind, the emotions, the whole person. Health is the amount of loving energy flowing through the being. The more the loving, the greater the health.

Using the techniques in this section—and all the others in the book, plus every technique you can gather from any other source—let that energy flow in you, through you.

When you think, "This is as healthy as I can possibly be!" add *et cetera* to it, and surrender even more to the flow of your self.

Health is not heavy. Health is light work.

God may forgive you,
but I never can.

ELIZABETH I
1533-1603

Of course God will forgive me;
that's his business.

HEINRICH HEINE
Last words
1856

For Giving

Forgiving means for giving—*for*, in favor of; *giving*, to give.

When you forgive another, who do you give to? The other? Sometimes. Yourself? Always. To forgive another is being *in favor of giving* to yourself.

In addition, most of us judge ourselves more harshly and more often than we judge others. It's important to forgive ourselves for all the things we hold against ourselves.

There is a third thing to forgive: the fact that we ever judged in the first place. When we judge, we leave our happiness behind—sometimes *way* behind. We know this, and we judge ourselves for having judged in the first place.

The layers of forgiveness, then, are two: first, the person we judged (ourselves or another); and, second, ourselves for having judged in the first place.

The technique? Simple. So simple, that some people doubt its effectiveness and don't try it. We urge you to try it. Try it for, say, five minutes and see what happens.

Say to yourself, "I forgive _____ (name of the person, place or thing you judged, including yourself) for _____ (the 'transgression'). I forgive myself for judging _____ (same person, place, or thing, including yourself) for _____ (what you judged)."

That's it. Simple, but amazingly effective. You can say it out loud, or say it to yourself. But, please, do say it.

If you have a lot to forgive one person for, you might want to invite that person into your sanctuary and forgive them there. (Ask your Master Teacher to come along, if you choose.)

That's all there is to forgiveness. Simple but powerful. How powerful? Give it five minutes. See what happens.

*Education is
what survives when
what has been learned
has been forgotten.*

B. F. SKINNER

For Getting

After you've forgiven the judgment, there's only one thing to do: forget it. Whatever "protection" you think you may gain from remembering all your past grievances is far less important than the balm of forgetting.

What's the value in forgetting? It's all in the word: for getting—to be in favor of getting, of receiving.

If you have a clenched fist, it is difficult to receive. If you let go and open the fist, you have a hand. Then it's easy to receive.

We sometimes think that shaking a fist (threateningly, with all the remembered transgressions) is the way to get something. A shaking fist tends to beget a shaking (or swinging) fist.

To receive, for give. To get, for get.

The space in your consciousness (mind, body, emotions) that's remembering a grievance is locked into remembering hurt, pain, anger, betrayal and disappointment. Who on earth wants to remember *that?* Let it go. *For give* it away. Then *for get* something new and better (light-er) in its place.

Heal the memories. Forgive the past. Then forget it. Let it go. It is not worth remembering. None of it's worth remembering. What's worth *experiencing* is the joy of this moment. Sound good?

To get it, for get.

*The children despise their
parents until the age of forty,
when they suddenly
become just like them
—thus preserving the system.*

QUENTIN CREWE

*My mother had
a great deal of trouble with me,
but I think she enjoyed it.*

MARK TWAIN

Parents

Just when we were feeling all joyful, did we have to bring *them* up? Well, they brought *us* up, so I guess we can bring *them* up.

It may seem that we have been harsh on parents in this book. When explaining why we tend to feel unworthy, think negatively, or aren't happy, we always seemed to return to the childhood, and there loomed mom and dad.

Yes, we are guilty of that, and now we make amends with these thoughts:

1. Your childhood is over. *You* are in charge of your life now. You can't blame the past, or anyone in the past, for what you do today. Even if you can formulate a convincing argument, it does you no good at all. It's gone. It's past.

Blaming the past is like blaming gravity for the glass you broke. Yes, without gravity, the glass would not have fallen and broken. But you *know* about gravity, and you *know* about glasses, and you *know* what happens when you combine gravity, a falling glass, and a floor.

Your childhood is like gravity. It was what it was. Your life today is like the glass. Handle it with care. If it breaks, it's nobody's fault. Clean up the mess, and get another glass from the cupboard.

2. Your parents did the best they could with what they knew. Like you, your parents weren't given an instruction manual for life. They had to learn it as they went along. They had to learn how to make a living, run a home, get along with each other, and raise a baby (you) all at the same time. No easy task. Along the way, they made lots of mistakes. They weren't the perfect parents. But, let's face it, you weren't the perfect child, either.

3. They gave you the greatest gift of all: Life. Whatever else they did or didn't do, if not for them, you wouldn't be here. They deserve a big thank you for that.

You don't have to *like* your parents. But it can help heal you if you learn to love them.

*Laughter is
inner jogging.*

NORMAN COUSINS

Laughter

Laugh. Out loud. Often.

Laughter's good for you, which may be too bad. If it raised the cholesterol count or had too many calories, people might do it more often.

If laughter were only *forbidden*, then people would do it all the time. The rebel yell would be replaced by the rebel yuck. They'd have laugh police. If they caught you laughing, they'd write you a ticket. Stand-up comics would become stand-up convicts. Sitcoms would be sitcons. Children's programming would have to be watched very carefully. We wouldn't want anyone pushing humor on young, innocent minds. "What are you kids doing in there?" "We're drinking beer and smoking cigarettes." "That's OK, but no laughing."

Considering how good laughter is for you, and how legal it is, we guess we should be thankful that it's as popular as it is.

Pop Quiz! Which of these lines is funniest:

(A) "I was gratified to be able to answer promptly. I said I don't know." (Mark Twain)

(B) "Aristotle was famous for knowing everything. He taught that the brain exists merely to cool the blood and is not involved in the process of thinking. This is true only of certain persons." (Will Cuppy)

(C) "The school of hard knocks is an accelerated curriculum." (Menander)

(D) "I knew I was an unwanted baby when I saw that my bath toys were a toaster and a radio." (Joan Rivers)

(E) "My parents put a live Teddy bear in my crib." (Woody Allen)

(F) "Never lend your car to anyone to whom you have given birth." (Erma Bombeck)

(G) Life is like laughing with a cracked rib.

Tears, idle tears,
I know not what they mean,
Tears from the depth of
some divine despair
Rise in the heart,
and gather to the eyes,
In looking on the happy
autumn fields,
And thinking of the days
that are no more.

ALFRED, LORD TENNYSON

1847

Tears

Crying, like laughing, is a marvelous, natural release. People feel *so good* after a cry, we wonder why it's so taboo.

People come pouring out of a movie, sniffling and dripping—you'd think they'd set off a tear gas canister in the theater. You ask them, "What happened?" fully expecting the story of a disaster. Between snivels, they sob, "That was the best movie I ever saw." (One wants to remind them that the correct grammar necessitates, "That was the best movie I *have* ever *seen*," but they seem to be upset enough already.)

Tears are a natural part of the healing process—and of the enjoyment process, as well. Intense feelings of gratitude, awe, and compassion are often accompanied by a swell of tears. "Moved to tears."

Allow yourself to be moved by life, not just the movies.

To live content
with small means;
to seek elegance rather than
luxury, and refinement
rather than fashion;
to be worthy,
not respectable,
and wealthy, not rich;
to study hard, think quietly,
talk gently, act frankly;
to listen to stars and birds,
to babes and sages,
with open heart;
to bear all cheerfully,
do all bravely, await
occasions, hurry never.
In a word, to let
the spiritual,
unbidden and unconscious,
grow up through
the common.
This is to be my symphony.

WILLIAM HENRY CHANNING
1810-1884

Wealth

Unlike money, wealth is not just what you have. Wealth is what you can do without.

Who is wealthier, the person who is addicted to something and has plenty of money to buy it, or the person who doesn't desire the addictive substance at all?

Wealthy people carry their riches within. The less they need of this physical world, the wealthier they are. They may or may not have large sums of money. It matters not. Whatever they have is fine.

Wealth is contentment, joy, balance, equanimity, inner peace.

Wealth is enjoying one's own company.

Wealth is being able to love oneself fully.

*Don't go to piano bars
where young, unemployed
actors get up and sing.
Definitely don't <u>be</u> a young,
unemployed actor who
gets up and sings.*

TONY LANG

Sacrifice

You would be far happier if you gave up certain things. This may not be easy for you. We nonetheless suggest you give them up—go cold turkey—starting right now, this minute, before you turn the page.

Give is an up word. *Up* is an up word. Put them together, and people get awfully down. "I'm not going to give up *anything*. And *sacrifice*. That's even *worse* than giving up. Sacrifice means giving up something *really* good."

The things we think you'd be better off sacrificing are things such as greed, lust, hurt, judgments, demands, spoiledness, envy, jealousy, vindictiveness.

Did you think we were going to ask you to give up *good* stuff? Most people think that sacrifice means giving up only the good stuff. Not so. The negative stuff, the cold stuff, the hard stuff—you can sacrifice those, too.

And you can give them *up*. Surrender them to the higher part of yourself. Surround them with light. Let them go.

You don't need them anymore.

The Sea of Galilee
and the Dead Sea are
made of the same water.
It flows down,
clear and cool,
from the heights of Hermon
and the roots of
the cedars of Lebanon.
The Sea of Galilee
makes beauty of it,
for the Sea of Galilee
has an outlet. It gets to give.
It gathers in its riches that
it may pour them out again
to fertilize the Jordan plain.
But the Dead Sea with the
same water makes horror.
For the Dead Sea
has no outlet.
It gets to keep.

HARRY EMERSON FOSDICK
The Meaning of Service
1920

Service

The idea that life is take, take, take (learn, learn, learn) needs to be balanced with the idea that life is also giving (teaching). Receiving and giving, learning and teaching are two aspects of a single flow, not unlike breathing in (receiving) and breathing out (giving). One cannot take place without the other.

We inhale oxygen and exhale carbon dioxide. Plants absorb the carbon dioxide and release oxygen. The cycle is complete. This interconnectedness between giving and receiving is fundamental to life.

What is waste to animals is essential to plants, and vice versa. Our own taking from and giving to life is just as intimately connected.

As humans, we seem to be the students of the people who know more than we do, doers with the people who know just about as much as we do, and teachers of the people who know less than we do. Life is a process of learning, doing and teaching.

In ten minutes on the job, you may learn how to transfer a call on the new phone system, consult with a co-worker on a method for increasing sales, and teach someone how to load paper into the copy machine. And all this learning-doing-teaching can take place with the same person.

This learning-doing-teaching happens in almost every area of life—and all three often happen simultaneously. The child we are teaching to read and write is, in the same moment, teaching us about innocence and wonder.

When we give a stranger directions, why do we feel so good? Because giving is a natural part of life. If we're lost and somebody puts us on the right track, that feels good, too. Receiving is a natural part of life.

Sometimes the interplay is not as direct. Sometimes we receive from another—or group of others—for quite some time. There is no way to give back to them. They are serving us. It is their gift—not to us, but to themselves.

Boy: *Teach me what you know, Jim.*

Reverend Jim: *That would take hours, Terry. Ah, what the heck! We've all got a little Obi Wan Kenobie in us.*

TAXI

When we learn to give to ourselves so fully that our cup overflows, then we may be called to be of service.

Service is not a chore.

Service is a privilege.

In truth, giving is not just a natural act; when our cup runneth over, it hurts *not* to give. We see the pain in another, and, knowing the balm for that pain, we want to ease the hurting.

Sometimes we must not give, for to give would be to intrude. And sometimes—when we are lucky, when we are blessed—we are permitted to share what we have. In that moment, the cycle is complete. We return the gift to nature as it was given to us.

Sometimes it's a hug, or a kind word, or the right bit of information at the right moment. Perhaps it's a smile, or a sigh, or a laugh. And maybe you cry for them.

There is no need to seek students, just as there is no need to seek lessons. When the teacher is ready, the student appears.

When the server is ready, the service appears.

Tomorrow is the most
important thing in life.
Comes into us at midnight
very clean.
It's perfect when it arrives
and it puts itself
in our hands.
It hopes we've
learned something
from yesterday.

JOHN WAYNE

The Attitude of Gratitude

Gratitude comes from the root word *gratus*, which means pleasing. The obvious interpretation is that when you are pleased with something, you are grateful. A second interpretation—the more radical one, and therefore the one we prefer—is that when you are grateful, *then* you are pleased, not by the thing, but by the gratitude.

In other words, in order to feel pleased, be grateful.

We have so much to be grateful for. Alas, it's part of human functioning to take good things for granted. It's biological, actually. A part of our brain actually filters out anything that isn't hurtful, fearful or physically moving. In olden days, it helped our forebears separate the beasts from the rocks and the trees.

Today, this same device starts filtering out all the good things we have, almost as soon as we get them. After a week or month or year with something that initially was *wonderful*, we have grown accustomed to it. We take it for granted.

What to do? Counteract complacency. *Consciously* be grateful for the good in your life. Make lists. Have gratitude flings. Be thankful for little things, big things, every thing.

Appreciate the things that are so magnificent, you took them for granted decades ago. What are we talking about? Your senses. Quick! Name all five! Some people can name the five Great Lakes faster than name their own senses. Then there's the brain, and the body, and the emotions, and walking, talking, thumbs. Thumbs? Sure: Try to pick up some things without using your thumbs.

As Dale Evans once said, "I'm so busy loving *everybody*, I don't have any time to hate *anybody*." When you start noticing even a small portion of all there is to be grateful for, you'll find there's no leftover time to feel lack, hurt or want.

The attitude of gratitude: the great, full feeling.

*Happiness is having
a large, loving, caring,
close-knit family
in another city.*

GEORGE BURNS

It Takes Great Strength to Be Happy

Happiness is not easy. It's not for the weak, the timid, the wishy-washy, the easily dissuaded, or the uncertain.

Happiness is not for wimps.

Happiness requires courage, stamina, persistence, fortitude, perseverance, bravery, boldness, valor, vigor, concentration, solidity, substance, backbone, grit, guts, moxie, nerve, pluck, resilience, spunk, tenacity, tolerance, will power, chutzpah, and a good thesaurus.

If you think happiness is easy, think again. The *theory* of happiness is easy; so easy, in fact, it can be stated in a parenthesis ("to be happy, think happy thoughts") in the middle of a not-very-long sentence. The *practice* of that theory—the successful implementation of that theory—that's where the courage, stamina, etc., etc. come in.

Our lives are full of happy things we can think happy thoughts about. If we run out of those, there are lots of books full of happy thoughts. There are lots of other things full of happy thoughts, too. Go rent *The Sound of Music* again. All we have to do is focus on the happy things to think happy thoughts, which will make us happy. That's all.

THEN WHY THE HELL AREN'T WE HAPPY ALL THE TIME, DAMN IT!!??

(We will have a slight pause while one of the co-authors makes the other co-author some tea—and puts a mild sedative in it. He's been working hard, you know—but obviously not on happiness.)

Now, very quietly, we will continue. With the pressures and distractions we've already discussed—the Fight or Flight response, the inaccurate yet all-pervading feeling of unworthiness, habits, addictions, brain parts that filter out good stuff, and so on—it is little wonder that thinking happy thoughts all the time takes some, well, strength.

It also takes practice, and patience, and discipline. It's not an easy challenge, but when you're through, you'll know you've done your work and done it well. You'll be among the strong, the proud, the few.

Be all that you can be. Join the happy.

*If you don't like
what you're doing,
you can always
pick up your needle and
move to another groove.*

TIMOTHY LEARY

You Don't *Have* to Do Anything

Really. You don't. Well, yes, a few biological things, but for the most part, everything you do, you do because you're *choosing* to do it. You might as well admit that. At least to yourself. It makes life a lot easier.

When we were children (oh, no: not *childhood* again), if we didn't do the things we "had" to do, this might displease our parents, and they controlled the *food*. Today, you control the food—and the clothing, and the shelter, and all the necessary things for life.

"Have to" implies need, and need is food-shelter-clothing. Everything else is just a "want." Therefore, unless it's doing something to put a scrap of food in your mouth, a few rags on your back, or a temporary roof over your head, you don't *have to* do it.

All those things you think you *have* to do, you can tell yourself, "I don't have to_____," and fill in the blank. It's quite liberating. It feels good. Then if you *choose* to do the thing, that's fine.

You can add to it, "And what I choose to do, I can do." Because you can.

Learn the art of patience.

*Apply discipline
to your thoughts
when they become anxious
over the outcome of a goal.*

*Impatience breeds anxiety,
fear, discouragement
and failure.*

*Patience creates
confidence, decisiveness
and a rational outlook,
which eventually leads
to success.*

BRIAN ADAMS

Hurry Up and Be Patient!

The sooner you're patient, the easier your life will become. Really. When you're patient, you can relax and enjoy the ride. Life has its own timing. Although perfect, life often disagrees with human-created timetables.

You feel *so good* about life when you're patient. We would suggest that you not delay a moment. Obtain patience at your earliest possible opportunity. It makes obtaining everything else so much easier, and much more fun. And if you *don't* get all of what you want, that's OK, because you're patient.

Some people like to doctor around with life—they think they can "fix" it. Life doesn't need a doctor. It's not sick. As KungFucious say, "If you want to doctor life, maybe you need to be patient."

Speaking of doctors, have we told you of all the health problems that can be caused by impatience? No? Well, it's pretty depressing. And depression—that causes health problems, too. Do you know how much stress getting sick causes the body? A lot. People get sick from it. Yes, it's best to avoid all that. Your very life may depend on how quickly you can get patient.

Not that we want to rush you. Do it in your own time. We just hate to see anyone suffer needlessly. You can start by taking a deep breath—all the way down, into your lower abdomen. Hurry up and do it before you have to do something else so you can take your time. That's important. There. Doesn't that feel better? That's the beginning of patience.

Well, we don't want to write more than a page on patience, and we're running out of room. We hope we have impressed upon you the dire need to be patient. But there's no hurry. If you're impatient, be patient with that. Unless, of course, you have trouble enjoying the moment, in which case, rather than being patient with impatience, you might as well be patient with life, and we're running out of room for this chapter so we have to run now. By the way, the key to patience is acceptance. Thanks. Bye.

We are here and it is now.
Further than that,
all knowledge is moonshine.

H. L. MENCKEN

Live Now

What a strange title for a chapter. "Live Now." When else are we supposed to live? Now, of course. But many people spend a lot of time (that precious commodity for getting what you want) in the past—remembering things that happened, and being upset over them.

Other people spend a lot of time in the future, worrying about this, that and something else—most of which probably never comes to pass. (F.E.A.R. = False Expectations Appearing Real.)

Some people are bi-timers. They can say "bye" to the present and go zipping off into both the past *and* the future simultaneously.

What happened to the moment? No, don't answer that. You have to go back in the past to do so. What about *this* moment. Oops. Gone. It's easier to pick up quicksilver with no thumbs than to capture the moment.

So don't capture it. There's nothing to capture. It's all here—present, although perhaps slightly unaccounted for. There's nothing to struggle with. When you come back from the past or the future, the present will be here, waiting.

It won't be the *same* present, of course. As Heraclitus observed around 500 B.C. (talk about the past!), "You could not step twice into the same river; for other waters are ever flowing on to you." Thus it is with time.

The irony is that there's nowhere to go. It's all here, now, in the moment. The further irony is that you *can't* go anywhere, even if you tried. If you're in the "past" or the "future," you're not in those places at all. You're thinking and feeling about them—but you're thinking and feeling about the past and future *right now*. In the present.

We are, thus, always in the present, no matter what we do, no matter where we "go." If someone insists, "Come present!" tell them, "I was present—with my thoughts. If you do something more interesting than my thoughts, I'll pay attention to you." *That* should bring them present.

"Live Now." What a strange title for a chapter.

*She knows what is the
best purpose of education:
not to be frightened
by the best
but to treat it as
part of daily life.*

JOHN MASON BROWN

Worthiness

There is nothing you need to do to become worthy. You already are worthy. You don't even have to discover your worthiness. You can feel utterly worthless and still be worthy.

People have said, "I don't feel worthy to be alive." But you *are* alive, therefore you *must* be worthy. It's very simple: if you're not worth life, you don't have it.

Worthiness is a given. It has nothing to do with action, thoughts, feelings, mind, body, emotions or anything else. You are worthy because you *are*. Period. End of sentence. End of chapter.

*So much is a man worth
as he esteems himself.*

FRANÇOIS RABELAIS
1532

Worthiness, Part Two

"If I'm worthy just because I am, how come I don't *feel* worthy?"

You're not talking about worthiness. You're talking about *self-esteem*. If you want to think better about yourself and feel better about yourself, learn to improve your self-esteem.

"Where do I learn about self-esteem?"

Next chapter.

Ofttimes nothing
profits more
Than self-esteem,
grounded on
just and right
Well managed.

JOHN MILTON
1667

Self-Esteem

Self-esteem is how you think and feel about yourself—how you *regard* yourself.

If you were taught that you must be perfect, then your self-esteem might be pretty low—humans are notoriously not perfect. Or, maybe you were taught that everything you do and whatever you do is perfect, in which case, your self-esteem might be pretty high.

Increasing your self-esteem is easy. You simply do good things, *and remember that you did them.*

We put that last part in italics because that's where most people slip up. In fact, most people already *do* enough good things for some high-class self-esteem. Alas, people tend to *forget*. They do so much good, most of it's taken for granted and forgotten almost as soon as it's done. Some like to think of this as humility. We think of it as a cause of low self-esteem. (True humility is being truthful.)

Make a list of all the good things you do. Then review the list. Often. Take note of the often-overlooked good you do. Did you bathe in the past 48 hours? Very good. Brush your teeth, too? Terrific. Use deodorant? Excellent. You've done your part in the fight against indoor air pollution. Put those on your list.

Take note of your moment-by-moment life: the people you smile at, the pedestrians you stop for, the friends you support, the relatives you're nice to, the boss (or employees) you put up with. The list goes on and on.

Honestly—you're a pretty decent human being, aren't you? Of course you are. How do we know? Nasty, wicked, slug-like people don't read books such as this. If they do, they certainly don't get as far as page 361.

You're great—warm, witty, friendly, kind, compassionate. Now if you only had a better memory so you could remember all this without having to buy books to remind you, you'd be perfect!

*Sometimes
I sits and thinks,
and sometimes
I just sits.*

Meditate, Contemplate or "Just Sits"

In addition to visualization, you might like to try any number of meditative and contemplative techniques available—or you might just want to sit quietly and relax.

Whenever you meditate, contemplate or "just sits," it's good to ask the white light to surround, fill and protect you, knowing only that which is for your highest good and the highest good of all concerned will take place during your meditation.

Before starting, prepare your physical environment. Arrange not to be disturbed. Unplug the phone. Put a note on the door. Wear ear plugs if noises might distract you. (We like the soft foam-rubber kind sold under such trade names as E.A.R., HUSHER and DECIDAMP.) Take care of your bodily needs. Have some water nearby if you get thirsty, and maybe some tissues, too.

Contemplation is thinking *about* something, often something of an uplifting nature. You could contemplate any of the hundreds of quotes or ideas in this book. Often, when we hear a new and potentially useful idea, we say, "I'll have to think about that." Contemplation is a good time to "think about that," to consider the truth of it, to imagine the changes and improvements it might make in your life.

Or, you could contemplate a nonverbal object, such as a flower, or a concept, such as God. The idea of contemplation is to set aside a certain amount of quiet time to think about just *that*, whatever you decide "that" will be.

Meditation. There are so many techniques of meditation, taught by so many organizations, that it's hard to define the word properly. We'll give a capsule summary of some techniques from John-Roger's book, *Inner Worlds of Meditation*. (For more complete descriptions, you can get the book for $7 postpaid, from Mandeville Press, Box 3935, Los Angeles, CA 90051.)

You might want to try various meditations to see what they're like. With meditation, please keep in mind that *you'll never know until you do it*. We may somehow like to think we know what the effects of a given meditation

*What would you
attempt to do
if you knew
you could not fail?*

DR. ROBERT SCHULLER

will be by just reading the description, and that, in fact, is exactly what happens. We *think* we know; we don't *really* know. We suggest you try it, gain the experience, and decide from that more stable base of knowledge what is best for you at this time. And please remember to "call in the light" before beginning. We suggest you do not do these meditations while driving a car, operating dangerous machinery or where you need to be alert.

Breathing Meditation. Sit comfortably, close your eyes, and simply be aware of your breath. Follow it in and out. Don't "try" to breathe; don't consciously alter your rhythm of breathing; just follow the breath as it naturally flows in and out. If you get lost in thoughts, return to your breath. This can be a very refreshing meditation—twenty minutes can feel like a night's sleep. It's also especially effective when you're feeling emotionally upset.

Tones. Some people like to add a word or sound to help the mind focus as the breath goes in and out. Some people use *"one"* or God or AUM (OHM) or love. These—or any others—are fine. As you breathe in, say to yourself, mentally, "love." As you breathe out, "love." A few other tones you might want to try:

- **HU.** HU is an ancient sound for the higher power. One of the first names humans ever gave to a supreme being was HU. Some good words begin with HU: *humor, human, hub* (the center), *hug, huge, hue, humus* ("The Good Earth"), *humble,* and, of course, *hula.* HU is pronounced "Hugh." You can say it silently as you breathe in, and again as you breathe out. Or, you can pronounce the letter H on the inhale and the letter U on the exhale. You might also try saying HU out loud as you exhale, but don't do it out loud more than fifteen times in one sitting; the energies it produces can be powerful.

- **ANI-HU.** This tone brings with it compassion, empathy and unity. You can chant it silently (ANI on the inhale, HU on the exhale) or out loud (ANI-HU on the exhale). It makes a lovely group chant and tends to harmonize the group—in more ways than one.

This art of resting the mind
and the power of
dismissing from it
all care and worry
is probably
one of the secrets of energy
in our great men.

CAPTAIN J. A. HADFIELD

- **HOO.** This can be used like the HU. Some people prefer it. It's one syllable, pronounced like the word *who*.

- **RA.** RA is a tone for bringing great amounts of physical energy into the body. You can do it standing or sitting. Standing tends to bring in more energy. Take a deep breath and, as you exhale, chant, out loud, "ERRRRRRRRAAAAAAAAA" until your air runs out. Take another deep breath and repeat it; then again. After three RAs, breathe normally for a few seconds. Then do another set of three, pause, then another set of three. We suggest you don't do more than three sets of three at any one time.

- **SO-HAWNG.** The SO-HAWNG meditation is a good one to use when your mind wants to do one thing and your emotions another. SO-HAWNG tends to unify the two, getting them on the same track. This tone is done silently. You breathe in on SO and out on HAWNG. Try it with your eyes closed for about five minutes and see how you feel. You may feel ready to accomplish some task you've been putting off for a long time.

- **THO.** THO is a tone of healing. The correct pronunciation of it is important. Take a deep breath, and as you breathe out say, "THooooo." The TH is accented; it's a sharp, percussive sound (and it may tickle your upper lip). It's followed by "ooooooo" as an extended version of the word *oh*. To do the THO meditation, sit comfortably, close your eyes, inhale and exhale twice, take a third deep breath, and on the third exhale, say, "THoooooo." Repeat three times this series of three breaths with THO aloud on the third breath. That's enough. It's powerful. Feel the healing energies move through your body. You can also chant THO inwardly as a formal meditation or any time during the day, even while doing something else. (But, again, as with all meditations, not while driving a car or operating potentially dangerous equipment.)

Flame Meditation. This uses the power of fire to dissolve negativity. Put a candle on a table and sit so you

Your vision
will become clear
only when you can look
into your own heart.
Who looks outside, dreams;
who looks inside, awakes.

CARL JUNG

can look directly into the flame, not down on it. Allow your energy to flow *up* and *out* into the candle. You may feel negativity or have negative thoughts. Don't pay any attention to their content; just release them into the flame. If you feel your energy dropping back down inside of you as though you were going into a trance, blow out the candle and stop the meditation. The idea is to keep the energy flowing up and out and into the flame. Do it for no more than five minutes to start. See how you feel for a day or so afterward. You may have more vivid dreams. If you feel fine otherwise, you might try it for longer periods. Twenty minutes a day would be a lot.

Water Meditation. Take some water in a clear glass, hold it between your hands (without your two hands touching each other), and simply look down into the glass. Observe whatever you observe. You may see colors. You may see energy emanating from your hands. You may just see yourself holding a glass of water. Observe the water for five minutes, gradually working up to fifteen. Drink the water at the end of the meditation. Your energies have made it a "tonic," giving you whatever you may need at that time. As an experiment, you can take two glasses, each half-filled with tap water. Set one aside, and do the water meditation with the other. Then taste each. Don't be surprised if the one you "charged" tastes different.

E. The E sound is chanted out loud after meditation to "ground" you and bring your focus back to the physical. It's a steady "Eeeeeeeeeeeee" as though you were pronouncing the letter E. It begins at the lower register of your voice, travels to the upper range, then back down again in one breath. You begin as a bass, go through tenor, alto, onto soprano, and back to bass again. As you do this, imagine that the sound is in your feet when you're in the lower register, gradually going higher in your body as your voice goes higher, finally reaching the top of your head at the highest note of the eeee, and then back down your body as the voice lowers. If you try it, you'll see that it's far easier to do than it is to explain. Do two or three E sounds after each meditation session.

≈

Men stumble over the truth
from time to time,
but most pick themselves up
and hurry off
as if nothing happened.

SIR WINSTON CHURCHILL

These tones and meditations have worked for many people. We don't ask you to *believe* they work. We simply ask you, if you like, to try them and see what happens. If they do work, you don't need belief; you've got knowledge. Your results will dictate whether you'll use them often, sometimes, seldom or never. Some may work better for you than others; that's only natural. Use the ones that work best for you now and, every so often, return to the others to see if they will offer more.

Some people think meditation takes time *away* from physical accomplishment. Taken to extremes, of course, that's true. Most people, however, find that meditation *creates* more time than it *takes*.

Meditation is for rest, healing, balance and information. All these are helpful in the attainment of a goal. Here's an additional technique you might want to add to your meditation. It's designed to make both the meditation and the time outside of meditation more effective.

One of the primary complaints people have about meditating is, "My thoughts won't leave me alone." Perhaps the mind is trying to communicate something valuable. If the thought is something to do, write it down (or record it on a tape recorder). Then return to the meditation. This allows the mind to move onto something else— such as meditation, for example.

As the "to do" list fills, the mind empties. If the thought, "Call the bank," reappears, you need only tell the mind, "It's on the list. You can let that one go." And it will. (It is important, however, to *do* the things on the list—or at least to consider them from a nonmeditative state. If you don't, the mind will not pay any more attention to your writing it down than you do, and it will continue to bring it up, over and over.)

When finished meditating, not only will you have had a better meditation, you will also have a "to do" list that is very useful. One insight gleaned during meditation might save *hours*, perhaps *days* of unnecessary work. That's what we mean when we say—from a purely practical point of view—meditation can make more time than it takes.

First keep the peace
within yourself,
then you can also
bring peace to others.

THOMAS à KEMPIS

1420

Peace

Peace is the cessation of againstness.

If you want peace, stop fighting.

If you want peace of mind, stop fighting with your thoughts. Let them be. Let them think what they want to think. They're going to do it anyway. As long as your mind gives you enough focus to take the next step in the direction you want to go, then let it be.

If you want peace in your emotions, stop trying to control them. Feelings are there to feel. Let them feel. Take information from them as needed, and let them feel what they want to feel.

If you want physical peace, stop the struggle of life. Don't push the body beyond its fatigue point. Rest the body enough. Exercise it enough. Then let it be. Don't demand that it live up to every image of performance and physical perfection you think it should have.

If you want peace with others, don't fight them. Go your own way. Live your own life. If some walk with you, fine. If you walk alone for periods of time, fine. If you don't like what's going on somewhere, leave. Maintain a portable paradise within yourself. Move to that peaceful place when the first glimmer of a temptation to fight another appears.

This does not mean you have to *like* what's going on. "The lion shall lie down with the lamb." It does not say the lion shall make love to the lamb. If you know you have to lie down with the lamb, bring a good book. That will occupy your mind so you don't have to feel againstness toward the lamb—you don't have to think about the lamb at all.

When you're not against yourself or others, you are at peace.

Peace. Be still.

*Fortunate, indeed, is
the man who takes
exactly the right
measure of himself,
and holds a just balance
between
what he can acquire
and
what he can use,
be it great or be it small!*

PETER LATHAM
1789-1875

Balance

Have you noticed some contradictions in this book? So have we. Welcome to life.

Should we "get off our buts" and "do it," or should we "meditate, contemplate, just sits" and "accept" our current reality? Should we laugh or cry? Should we go for money or for wealth? Should we cling tight to this life, or should we look forward to death? Should we be flexible or firm? Assertive or accepting? Giving or receiving?

There is no one answer to any of these questions. It's a matter of time and timing, of seas and seasons, of breathing in and breathing out.

It's a matter of balance.

Balance is the point between the extremes. And yet, the point is always shifting, always moving. A successful life can be like a successful tightrope walk. Sometimes the balance pole dips violently one way, sometimes it dips gently the other. And sometimes it's perfectly still.

How does one find and maintain balance? Vigilance. Internal vigilance. Internal vigilance is the price of freedom.

When you notice an out-of-balance situation within yourself, balance it at once. If you don't, it will find a reflection outside. Then there's something "out there" to balance, too. It's easier to balance it within, before it gets out.

For balanced action, ask yourself, "What would a Master do?" Look through the eyes of a Master. Masters always perform "right action." Seeing as a Master sees, "What would a Master do?" Sometimes a Master would do nothing. Sometimes, quite a lot. "What would a Master do?" Do that.

You are a Master. You might as well get good at it.

*People think
love is an emotion.
Love is good sense.*

KEN KESEY

Loving

We speak of love in many different ways. When talking with psychologists, we call love, "Unconditional positive regard." When talking to the religious, we say, "God is love." When talking to religious psychologists, we might say, "Love is God's unconditional positive regard."

When we go within, we know that our core—our very being—is love. All we can do is share that love with ourselves and others; to make it a verb—loving—and do what we can to live in accordance with it.

Our loving is a work in progress. We are continuously refining it, honing it, adding to it, shaping it. This is what we *think* we are doing. We also know the reality is that love is continuously refining, honing, adding to, and shaping *us*.

We are doing our best to be students of love. At this point, we step down from the lectern and join you as classmates.

Writing this book was an act of loving. We genuinely wanted to communicate the ideas found here, because we find these ideas valuable. We know that reading this book was an act of loving on your part. People do not read books such as this without a fierce commitment to the love of self and others.

We wish we knew how to end this book. We are certainly capable of serving up some platitudes on love and calling it a day. But we've been honest with you thus far. We've written from our experiences—from our hearts to yours, we like to think.

What *do* we have to say about loving?

- *Loving* is an action. *Love* is a thing. ("The difference between love and loving, is the difference between fish and fishing," as the poet said.) We like *loving*—the moving, growing, changing, active, dynamic interplay (inner play?) between self and others, and between self and self.

- Loving starts with the individual. When we want loving from someone outside ourselves to "make us

*If you feel you have
both feet planted
on level ground,
then the university
has failed you.*

ROBERT F. GOHEEN

Gude nicht, and joy be wi' you a'.

CAROLINA OLIPHANT,
BARONESS NAIRNE
LIFE AND SONGS
1869

whole," we know we are not giving ourselves the loving we need.

- When we give ourselves the loving we need (and it takes so little time when we actually *do* it!), our time with others tends to be joyful, graceful, playful, touching and—in each moment—complete.

- Loving is the greatest teacher.

≈

This book cannot be wrapped up in a string and handed to you as a tidy package because, frankly, neither can life. Or loving. It's a process. Ongoing processes don't have tidy endings, merely transitions.

So welcome to the transitional chapter of this book. From this point, it's not a book to be *read* (you're within minutes of completing that), but a book to be *used*.

And we, to the degree that we have been "teachers," gladly hand the mantle over to your Master Teacher. We are content to become reference librarians—here when you need to research questions such as "How am I supposed to use guilt as a friend?" "What was this about using relationships as a mirror?" or "Didn't they say something about *money?*"

It's been good taking this journey with you. Thank you for joining us—or letting us join you. *LIFE 101* now makes the transition from a book that leads, to a book you can carry.

Take good care. School is still in session. The surprise continues.

Enjoy.

For Further Study: Organizations Founded by John-Roger

This is Peter, stepping out of my co-author character to tell you about some of the organizations founded by John-Roger.

J-R must like founding organizations. I certainly *hope* he likes founding organizations—he's founded enough of them. It's probably more accurate to say that organizations formed around John-Roger; he stands still for a while and teaches, and the people listening to him form organizations by which these teachings can be shared with others.

The organizations range from secular to the spiritual—that is, some are of The Gap, and some are not. I'll list them in approximate order of Gap-ness—starting with the purely secular.

Now that you've had a taste of J-R's teachings (through this book), you might like to explore some more. (In this book we have barely scratched the surface—he's been at it nonstop for the past 27 years.)

I'll be brief. You might want to ask your Master Teacher which, if any, of these you might like to pursue.

Insight Seminars provides workshops on personal development. The flagship seminar—and a great place to start—is Insight I, The Awakening Heart Seminar. Insight Seminars are offered in dozens of cities all over the world. I can't recommend them too highly. Insight Seminars, 2101 Wilshire Blvd., Santa Monica, CA 90403; 213-829-9816 or 800-777-7750.

The Center Store carries a broad range of books, tapes, and other educational materials on personal growth. You might ask about the book *One Minute Self-Esteem,* or the book/tape package *250 Ways to Enhance Your Self-Esteem,* both by Candy Semigran. The Center Store also carries a series of audio tapes by John-Roger. Please contact the store for more information about their full line of products. Center Store, 2101 Wilshire Blvd., Santa Monica, CA 90403; 213-453-0071 or 800-344-4976.

The Heartfelt Foundation is dedicated to service. They do various community projects, large and small, all over the world. If you'd like to take part—or organize a service project in your community—give them a call. 2101 Wilshire Blvd., Santa Monica, CA 90403; 213-828-0535.

Institute for Individual and World Peace. Just as it says. If you want to learn more about peace and how you can effect it—or if you have any ideas to contribute—drop them a line. 2101 Wilshire Blvd., Santa Monica, CA 90403; 213-828-0535.

University of Santa Monica. Offering an M.A. in Applied Psychology, including the Awakening the Inner Counselor program. Approved by the State of California. Write or call for a brochure. 2107 Wilshire Blvd., Santa Monica, CA 90403; 213-829-7402.

University of Santa Monica Center for Health. A gathering of health professionals dedicated to treating the patient, not just the symptoms. They work toward both the elimination of illness and the enhancement of wellness. They also have a division, the Santa Monica Institute for Stress Related Disorders. Call or write for a brochure. 2105 Wilshire Blvd., Santa Monica, CA 90403; 213-829-0453.

(Those organizations that would be classified as Gap-like begin here.)

Movement of Spiritual Inner Awareness (MSIA) is for those who want to live in a way that makes spirit and God a part of their lives. MSIA has no formal membership, dues, rules or dogma. It encourages people in their own experience of the divine, without restricting personal choices. The booklet "About MSIA" describes MSIA and its goals. You can also find out if J-R's TV show "That Which Is" is available in your area. Write or call MSIA, Box 3935, Los Angeles, CA 90051; 213-737-4055.

Discourses. John-Roger's Soul Awareness Discourses are the most complete, effective and delightful course in Spirit I know. You simply read one a month at your own pace. Each Discourse contains about 30 pages of text and more than 60 blank pages for your own daily notes, reminders, dreams, discoveries, affirmations or anything else you'd like. They're $100 per year (12 Discourses), and I can't recommend them too highly. For more information, please contact MSIA.

Mandeville Press. Publishes J-R's earlier books, including *Relationships—The Art of Making Life Work, The Power Within You,* and *Wealth and Higher Consciousness*. On a more spiritual note, there's *Loving...Each Day, The Spiritual Promise, The Spiritual Family* and *The Way Out Book*. Other books are available. They also publish *The New Day Herald,* a bi-monthly newspaper of articles on, mostly, loving. A vast collection of John-Roger on audio and video tapes is available, looking at life from a spiritual yet practical point of view. A free catalog is available from MSIA.

Other Books (and Stuff) Published by Prelude Press

This is still Peter. I thought I'd tell you about some of the books published by Prelude Press. This may seem like a shameless commercial. It is not. As author (or co-author) and publisher of these books, I say it's not a commercial—it is an exercise in blatant egoism.

LIFE 101 Audio Tapes

A new recording of the entire text of this book (no abridgements here) read by Academy Award nominee Sally Kirkland, Christopher McMullen, Yours Truly and a cast of dozens. (All right, so they're no dozens.) Five tapes, $19.99

LIFE 101 Watch

A Paul LeBus designed wristwatch with all the color and fun of the cover of *LIFE 101*. The words on the watch face read "Time to enjoy...LIFE 101." $35. One size fits most. (If you want to see what the watch looks like, please see the cover of the book *DO IT!* at your local bookstore.)

DO IT! Let's Get Off Our Buts

DO IT! is a book for those who want to discover—clearly and precisely—their dream; who choose to pursue that dream even if it means learning (and—gasp!—practicing) new behavior; who wouldn't mind having some fun along the way; and who are willing to expand their comfort zone enough to include their heart's desire—and maybe even a dance floor. Hardcover. 500 pages. $20.

DO IT! Audio Tapes

Every word of the book, read by Sally Kirkland, Christopher McMullen and Yours Truly (I do the quotes). Six tapes, $22.99.

You Can't Afford the Luxury of a Negative Thought

This is the first book John-Roger and I co-authored. In its 622 pages, we've done all that we can to make a "serious" subject (life-threatening illness) light. As we point out in the introduction, "This is not just a book for people with life-threatening illnesses. It's a book for anyone afflicted with one of the primary diseases of our time: negative thinking." Trade paperback, $15.00.

Focus on the Positive: The You Can't Afford the Luxury of a Negative Thought Workbook

By John-Roger and Peter McWilliams. Specific exercises to help you eliminate the negative and latch onto the affirmative. Trade paperback, $12.

Index

About the Authors

JOHN-ROGER, an educator, has been very busy during the past twenty-seven years. He has traveled the world, teaching, lecturing, writing and presenting seminars on just about every conceivable area of personal growth. He founded several organizations dedicated to a broad range of projects including health, education, spirit, philosophy, service, integrity, corporate excellence and individual and world peace. He has written twenty-five books, recorded hundreds of audio and video tapes, and has a nationally syndicated television show, *That Which Is.*

PETER McWILLIAMS published his first book, a collection of poetry, at the age of seventeen. His series of poetry books went on to sell more than 3,000,000 copies. A book he co-authored on meditation was #1 on the New York Times best-seller list. He is the co-author of *How to Survive the Loss of a Love.* His *The Personal Computer Book* was a best-seller. He is a nationally syndicated columnist, teaches seminars, and has appeared on the *Oprah Winfrey Show, Donahue, Larry King* and *The Today Show.*

*If you would like to receive
information about future
books, tapes, lectures, etc.
by John-Roger and
Peter McWilliams,
please send
your name and address
to:*

*Prelude Press
8165 Mannix Drive
Los Angeles, California
90046*

Thank you.